"Though we often do whatever it takes to avoid feelings of loneliness, in these pages Dr. Kelly Flanagan invites readers to do something else—make friends with our loneliness, attend to it, and even welcome loneliness as a gift. Flanagan is a guide for the isolated soul, showing us that our agonizing longings for deep companionship are actually graces—signposts pointing us toward deeper connection, love, and holiness. And along the way, we discover this gentlest of miracles: we are, none of us, truly alone."

Aubrey Sampson, church planter and author of *The Louder Song: Listening for Hope in the Midst of Lament*

"In *True Companions*, Kelly Flanagan grapples with the joys and risks of genuine connection. With sincerity, wisdom, and deft storytelling, Flanagan dares readers to become more human. In an increasingly inhumane world, his is a dare worth taking."

Katherine Willis Pershey, author of *Very Married: Field Notes on Love and Fidelity*

"I know this book will touch many lives. Kelly Flanagan has harvested the rich rewards of true companionship from the everyday struggles of doing real life together—a gift to every couple and every kind of companion everywhere."

Bob Goff, author of *Love Does* and *Dream Big*

"What a brave, beautiful, and bountiful book that sings with quiet wisdom on the power of loneliness and the sanctity of companionship. . . . Flanagan looks directly into the center of what it means to be human and helps us hold our gaze there, too, so we may see ourselves and each other more clearly with a searing and soaring grace."

Carolyn Weber, professor and author of *Sex and the City of God*

"Loneliness is part of marriage. Rather than avoid or ignore that reality, Flanagan provides a much-needed resource on the necessary journey of creating space for loneliness in the context of relationship. With unflinching honesty and clinical insight, Flanagan takes a fresh look at how to sit with the discomfort of unmet expectations in marriage. He shares about his own marriage in a way that impacts both intellectually and emotionally. Flanagan wisely suggests that our most intimate relationships benefit from learning to embrace curiosity rather than certainty, and that a deeper intimacy is found in sharing loneliness rather than expecting our partner to eliminate it."

Jeff and Kim Eckert, psychologists and cofounders of
Roots Counseling Center

"He had me at the table of contents. I went there first to decide if I was going to read the book. Weary of reading marriage books that seemed too lofty or talked about having a date night, I long ago moved on to books of poetry and novels, which have actually helped my marriage. But when I felt a tug at my heart just by reading the descriptions of the chapters in *True Companions*, I knew this book would be different. If you want a wise, honest, and true friend to take a walk with you, Kelly is that friend. And on that walk, he will open your heart to new truths and new questions, and gently lead you down an unexpected path toward change in yourself and your relationship with the one you love. Please take this journey with him. Kelly is a trustworthy guide."

Al Andrews, founder and executive director of Porter's Call

FOREWORD BY IAN MORGAN CRON

KELLY FLANAGAN

TRUE
COMPANIONS

A BOOK FOR EVERYONE ABOUT THE

RELATIONSHIPS THAT SEE US THROUGH

An imprint of InterVarsity Press
Downers Grove, Illinois

InterVarsity Press
P.O. Box 1400, Downers Grove, IL 60515-1426
ivpress.com
email@ivpress.com

InterVarsity Press® is the book-publishing division of InterVarsity Christian Fellowship/USA®, a movement of students and faculty active on campus at hundreds of universities, colleges, and schools of nursing in the United States of America, and a member movement of the International Fellowship of Evangelical Students. For information about local and regional activities, visit intervarsity.org.

All Scripture quotations, unless otherwise indicated, are taken from The Holy Bible, New International Version®, NIV®. Copyright © 1973, 1978, 1984, 2011 by Biblica, Inc.™ Used by permission of Zondervan. All rights reserved worldwide. www.zondervan.com. The "NIV" and "New International Version" are trademarks registered in the United States Patent and Trademark Office by Biblica, Inc.™

While any stories in this book are true, some names and identifying information may have been changed to protect the privacy of individuals.

Published in association with Creative Trust Literary Group LLC, 320 Seven Springs Way, Suite 250, Brentwood, TN 37027, www.creativetrust.com.

Author photo by Grot Imaging Studio, grotis.com.

Cover design and image composite: David Fassett
Interior design: Jeanna Wiggins
Images: dust scratches on a black background: © golubovy / iStock / Getty Images Plus
    botanical illustration: © bauhaus1000 / DigitalVison Vectors / Getty Images
    white texture background: © R.Tsubin / Moment Collection / Getty Images

ISBN 978-0-8308-4768-6 (print)
ISBN 978-0-8308-4769-3 (digital)

Printed in the United States of America ♾

InterVarsity Press is committed to ecological stewardship and to the conservation of natural resources in all our operations. This book was printed using sustainably sourced paper.

Library of Congress Cataloging-in-Publication Data
A catalog record for this book is available from the Library of Congress.

P 25 24 23 22 21 20 19 18 17 16 15 14 13 12 11 10 9 8 7 6 5 4 3 2 1
Y 42 41 40 39 38 37 36 35 34 33 32 31 30 29 28 27 26 25 24 23 22 21

A miracle is when the whole is greater than the sum of its parts. A miracle is when one plus one equals a thousand.

FREDERICK BUECHNER

CONTENTS

PART 3
GROW OLD—Cherishing Your Time

FOREWORD

Ian Morgan Cron

I F YOU'VE EVER GOTTEN THE BOTTOM of your shoes sticky walking on the caramel-popcorn-and-cotton-candy-strewn grounds of a carnival, you've seen or played a Whack-a-Mole game. The object is to get as high a score as possible by whacking as many moles as you can while they're popping up out of five holes in a huge wooden box. At first, their plastic heads rise up out of the holes slowly enough that you can whack that mallet like Thor with his hammer. But as the pace speeds up, the moles pop up and down faster and faster until you're in such a frenzy that the mallet is about to fly out of your grip.

As a kid, I learned to manage my feelings by whacking them as soon as they began to show up. If I was fast enough, I could make them disappear before I felt them—or worse, before I incurred the consequences of expressing them. Growing up, I learned that with enough whacks I could make sure that some of them would just stay down there (it never hurt to add a little substance-induced oblivion just to make sure), thank you very much.

That worked until it worked against me. I thought I was doing fine—well into sobriety; married to my college sweetheart; living in an idyllic yellow house in New Canaan, Connecticut; discovering my sweet spot in a growing ministry vocation; burying my father and, along with him (so I thought), the pesky demons that had colored my relationship with him so darkly. Whaddya know, those moles decided it was safe enough to pop back up again. This time I couldn't whack them—I didn't even have a mallet ready—and lickety-split went from zero to frenzy. "What is happening to me?" I asked my therapist. His answer gave me the vocation I've been on ever since: "You're waking up."

You don't have to read far into this lyrical book that Kelly Flanagan has sung into stunning form to realize that he's been schooled by his own version of Whack-a-Mole. There's nothing like flinging yourself irrevocably into a lifelong relationship with another human being to guarantee it will stir up the moles you'd managed to keep underground so long you forgot they were there. (His stories about his kids show that becoming a parent is another sure-fire invitation to raise the moles from your dead zones.)

What Kelly does for all of us in this deep dive into being-in-relation is help us unearth those deeply buried conditions we've been loading onto what we think we've been asking for or offering as "unconditional love." Then, therapist that he is, Dr. Flanagan invites us to put down the mallet and befriend our loneliness, shame, and abandonment. Those are the fears fueling our worst selves, whose job it is to keep us on autopilot. Kelly charts a path of waking up so we can show up as our best selves in our most important relationships.

Friends keep one another company. True companions keep each other tethered—to the ground of reality, to the ground of our being. Are you in a season of discovering that what used to work for (both of) you is now working against (both of) you? Been there, done that. It's why I'm so glad to commend *True Companions* to you—it comes with some really great strings attached.

WHAT YOU
NEED TO KNOW

I REALIZE NOW HOW VERY BRAVE and a little foolish it all really was.

On an otherwise ordinary afternoon in the autumn of 2001, I waited for her to walk down the aisle and join me at the altar. Twelve hours earlier, I'd awoken in the muted hours before dawn to transport a special bottle of champagne from my hotel to the office of our limo company. I had been mostly alone on the vacant highways. I'd done this by myself because it never occurred to me to ask for help. In those days, I was used to traveling through life alone.

Alone was all I'd ever known.

Then the doors opened and there she was, moving toward me. Time has taken from memory most of what followed, but I can still clearly remember how *happy* she looked walking down that aisle. Somehow I knew her happiness wasn't about her big day having finally arrived. She's not a center-of-attention kind of person, and she's not a waiting-for-prince-charming kind of woman. Rather, I knew her happiness was simply about marrying me. On the surface, I acted like this made perfect sense. I liked to pretend—even to myself sometimes—that I was quite a catch. However, underneath the bravado I was still confused about why a woman like her would tether herself to a guy like me.

Then, she was there. Next to me. *With* me. And in the moments that followed, I pledged the remainder of my life to her. Wedding vows are a little startling, if you are paying any kind of attention at all. I promised I'd stick by her through all sorts of catastrophe—poverty, illness, her death, or mine. Just a few weeks earlier, the Twin Towers had been reduced to a tragic pile of steel and stone. The rubble was still smoldering as my bride and I promised to stick by each other through buildings falling and bodies failing. To promise that kind of no-matter-whatness when you are twenty-some years old and living in a world on fire, you have to be a little foolish or a lot courageous. I think there was a bit of both in our vows that day. Yet, my wedding-day promise was not nearly the bravest thing I'd ever said to her.

Nine months after our first date, I had confessed to her for the first time.

Until then, I'd mostly just been putting on a show, trying hard to look confident, calm, and collected on the outside. Meanwhile, on the inside, the deep reservoir of anxiety I'd managed to keep hidden within me for most of my life was beginning to rise. The dam was breaking, and some of the anxiety was leaking out through my body. For instance, the inside of my mouth was so plagued by stress-induced cold sores I could barely eat with her, let alone kiss her. I'd kept her oblivious to all of it, though, because I was pretty sure "cold sores" was not one of the boxes she hoped to check in her search for a companion.

Then one morning, the dam finally broke for good. I decided I couldn't hide my suffering any longer. I sat her down, and with my head in my hands, I wept while telling her the truth. It was the bravest thing I'd ever done, to risk losing who I loved by being who I was. Again, time has washed away most of my memory about how all that truth flowed out of me. What I *do* remember is how she filled me back up with four little words: "We'll figure it out." It was the first vow she ever made to me, and it was, I think, my first taste of true companionship. A month later I started shopping for a ring. By the end of the summer we were engaged, and a little more than a year later we were standing at that altar, making promises that are awfully complicated to keep.

ABOUT THIS BOOK

When I began writing this book, I thought it was about saving this ancient institution called marriage. Seriously. I planned to right this sinking ship we call matrimony by convincing a whole generation of young people to quit jumping ship, to head to the courthouse, and to set sail upon the kind of life-changing journey marriage can become. Plus, "marriage books" sell like hotcakes. It all seemed like a very good idea.

Then, one day, a friend pushed back.

She asked about my next book, and when I told her what it was about, her face fell. "I love your writing," she explained, "but I can't pick up any book with marriage on the cover." She is a single woman. Men have been cruel to her. An uninterested father. A boyfriend who abandoned her in the middle of a pregnancy. A husband who drank their marriage to death. Now, she has the courage to stand alone while raising her young daughter on her own. She still hopes to marry again, but she has become less willing to settle for more of the same from the men in her life. In other words, for now, she doesn't have a ticket for the marriage cruise, and she isn't interested in reading about the poolside piña coladas.

I can't blame her. So, I wrote this book for her and for everyone like her. It's a book about a cruise we are, all of us, already on. This is a book about marriage that is also about something *bigger* than marriage. In her Pulitzer Prize–winning novel, *Gilead*, Marilynne Robinson writes, "The moon looks wonderful in this warm evening light, just as a candle flame looks beautiful in the light of morning. Light within light. . . . It seems to me to be a metaphor for the human soul, the singular light within the great general light of existence. Or it seems like poetry within language. Perhaps wisdom within experience. Or marriage within friendship and love." What if marriage is a singular light within the great general light of *companionship*, but we keep trying to turn it into the big light itself? What if uncovering the secrets to a stellar marriage isn't as important as finding our way to the truths at the heart of true companionship? This book is about the great general light of companionship, inside which marriage flickers and flames.

If I could, I'd go back in time and join my younger self in the early morning hours of his wedding day. I'd ride with him on that empty highway, with that bottle of champagne resting on the seat between us, and I'd tell him things he couldn't possibly fathom yet. I'd tell him marriage is relatively simple. It's a signature on a license at the courthouse, a benediction from the pastor, a kiss, a bunch of rice stuck in hair he won't have for much longer, a rowdy reception, and years and anniversaries rolling by, until one day the rolling finally stops.

But, I'd tell him, *companionship* is something he already began, on a painful morning of confession months before. I'd tell him companionship is anything but simple. It's hard work. It takes guts and perseverance. It's a long walk through *everything*: sorrow and celebration, heartbreaking disappointment and heartwarming contentment, all sorts of uncertainty and a moment of clarity here and there. It takes everything you've got, and sometimes it gives you back more than you could ever hope for. It is a four-word vow lived out in the midst of our hardest humanity:

We'll figure it out.

I'd tell him marriage is one very special candle that can burn within the big, bright light of companionship. Friendship is another one, of course, as is the relationship between a parent and a child, or the relationship between siblings. Really, wherever two or more are gathered, a little more light can be added to the great general light of companionship. I'd tell him he has spent much of his life thinking about how to get better at marriage and that might make him better at being married, but getting better at *companionship* will make him better at being *human*.

Then, he'd drop off the champagne at the limo office, where the lone attendant will look at him like he's nuts, and we'd drive back to the hotel together. On the way, I'd be sure to tell him what I witnessed last Thanksgiving Day in a buffet line at a local inn. While someone ahead of me contemplated corn versus carrots, I had time to stand there with an empty plate and observe, through two panes of glass, the line moving a little more quickly on the other side of the buffet.

What I saw was two companions.

I'm guessing they were in their early seventies, but something had happened to him. A stroke perhaps, or something nearly as catastrophic. His age was seventy-something, but his body was ninety-something. He slouched heavily with both hands on a walker in front of him, inching it forward with great effort, muscle tone almost completely missing. Large hearing aids were perched in both ears. With both hands on his walker, he was unable to reach for his own food. So she walked behind him, reaching for both of them.

They were figuring it out.

I watched as they slowly moved by the mashed potatoes and the stuffing and a bowl full of something made of marshmallows. She would serve herself and then lean over, with her mouth close to his ears, pointing at each pile of food, asking him if he wanted it. Sometimes he would nod. Sometimes he wouldn't. Slowly, his plate filled up. It was all very hushed. I could not hear a word of it. Usually, companionship isn't loud and fancy and intoxicating like a wedding celebration. It's quiet and plodding and nourishing. I'd tell my younger self that I don't know if the couple was married. They probably were. But I *do* know they were companions.

ABOUT UNCONDITIONAL LOVE

By then, we'd probably be pulling back into the hotel. He'd have vows to finish writing and would be eager to get on with his day, but I'd ask him to linger with me just a little longer. There's one more thing I need to tell him. It's about love. It will probably shock him, but that's why he needs to hear it. It's too counterintuitive and too important to be left unsaid. I'd start out by telling him about a fight he's going to have with his bride—seventeen years in the future.

It was less like a lovers' quarrel and more like an American Civil War battle, the kind where you declare a ceasefire at sundown, go back to your tents for the night, and resume in the morning after breakfast—the kind of fight that can last for a week, or weeks. It all started when she pointed out that I was "checking out." Around bedtime—when the kids most long for a father to come to them and see them and send them into their sleep—I was scrolling through my phone, checking email, returning texts, catching up on news, getting lost down YouTube rabbit holes. Basically, she told me I was digitally abandoning my family.

What I *heard* her say, though, was that I wasn't doing enough. So, I made a list of everything I had done for the family that week. Nothing was too big or too small to be included. Then, I went to my computer, and I typed it out. I actually did that. With differently sized fonts, some items boldfaced, some italicized, like I was preparing a proposal to a board of directors. After the kids were all in bed, I handed her the list.

Cue Gettysburg.

For about a week, I used my words like bayonets, and her eyes were muskets. Neither one of us was willing to retreat. She insisted bedtime books were not too much to ask from a dad who writes blogs and books about being an attentive father, and I refused to hear it as anything but unfair criticism. Eventually, one morning, we went on a long walk—so we could battle in front of our neighbors rather than our kids—and we reached a truce. Once all the treaties were signed, I was eventually able to identify the culprit behind the whole conflict.

Unconditional love.

Our fight had started because she had not loved me unconditionally. There were limitations to what she would put up with. Things I do she'd like to see stop. Things I don't do she'd like to see begin. Expectations for how I will act and live and love. *Conditions*, if you will, for her approval. I had called her out on her conditionality, and she had called me out on defending myself with high-minded ideas arising less from my desire to be perfectly loved than from my desire to be loved *as if I am perfect*. Sometimes, I'll fight a whole war before admitting she is right.

Of course, aspiring to unconditional love is a noble thing. Sitting in that parking lot on his wedding day, I'd want my younger self to know I'm not trying to undo anything he's learned in church or anywhere else about unconditional love. I firmly believe unconditional love is that from which we came and that to which we will return. What I'm suggesting is, noble things in human hands can quickly become not-so-noble. What I'm saying is, we don't need anyone to undo what we've been taught about unconditional love, because *we* undo it ourselves, oftentimes *while* we are being taught it. When our pastor or priest or whoever has the pulpit in our life begins talking about unconditional love, we often begin tweaking the ideas in favor of our justification rather than our *transformation*. We often use it to make love easier instead of truer.

For instance, we often hide our failures, flaws, and foibles behind it, demanding to be loved unconditionally under conditions no one should be expected to tolerate, let alone love. Or, in the name of loving someone unconditionally, we tend to forgive and forget things that should be confronted and condemned. We circumvent conflict and cut corners on the hardest parts of cultivating companionship because conflict scares us and corners cost us, and then we call those shortcuts unconditional love. Or, rather than engaging in the hard work of loving hard people, we steer clear of them, piously "accept" them, pat ourselves on the back for being tolerant, and congratulate ourselves for loving unconditionally. The thing about unconditional love—the thing that makes it something less than the cure-all we often want it to be—is that it can happen from *very, very far away*. From somewhere up in the heavens even.

Yet, not even God acted as if that kind of love was sufficient for true relationship. Even God decided unconditional love lacked something a little more proximal, something like skin, something like a body and a heartbeat and a pulse, something like a voice to bless with and a voice to berate with, something like arms for embracing each other and fingers for pointing *at* each other. Even God knew he had to come closer to us than unconditional love would require of him. So, on a silent night in a little town called Bethlehem, he did. In a manger, love came close.

I'm guessing my younger self would be all ears now, his unfinished vows forgotten for the moment. I'd ask him if he can see how easy it is to make unconditional love into an easy thing. He'd nod. I'd tell him he'll be tempted again and again to use unconditional love as a cop-out. I'd encourage him to choose something more *engaged* than unconditional love. Something *closer*. Something with molecules and guts and grit in it. He'd ask me what that something might be. And I'd tell him about his future son's bedroom.

Several months after our Gettysburg week, my wife asked me to join her at the doorway to our son Quinn's room. I peered in with her, and I saw a half-dozen odorous, preteen socks strewn across the floor, a basket of clean clothes that had been toppled and tossed across the room, a LEGO creation that had been demolished and spread underfoot, and a mad mishmash of other odds and ends. As we gazed upon the carnage, she said, with an equal mixture of wonder and anger, that she had ordered him to clean it up, and he had implied the mission was accomplished. I stood there with her, surveying the spectacle, not understanding her purpose in calling me to her. I asked her if she wanted help cleaning it up. No, she said, that's his job. Did she want me to give him consequences for ignoring her and—kinda sorta—lying to her? No, she said, she had started this and she could finish it.

So, we stood in silence and stared at it. I saw empty candy wrappers, a glass full of something rancid, a desiccated apple core, and the home phone that had gone missing a couple of days earlier. After a few more moments of silence, I finally asked the question, "Why did you want me here?"

Without taking her eyes off the mess, she put her arm around me and responded, simply, "I just wanted you to witness it with me." Her words made me recall something I'd been reading about and sharing with her. In English, we have only one word for love, but in the Greek language there are four words for love: *agape*, *eros*, *storge*, and *philia*.

Agape love is unconditional and often considered the highest and most noble love in the Greek language. It is the kind of love that keeps on loving even when the other is cruel, offensive, or unresponsive. It is sacrificial, in the sense that it will persist no matter what. It is the kind of love we have come to expect from a loving God, and in the Greek language it is used almost exclusively to describe being divine, not being human.

Eros, on the other hand, is sort of the opposite. Whereas *agape* is steadfast and enduring, *eros* is passionate and more fleeting. *Eros* is about chemistry and desire. It is the delightful euphoria in any budding romance. Over time, though, its energy cannot be sustained. When it is balanced by other kinds of love, it recedes into the depths of a relationship, arising more occasionally during punctuated moments of merging. However, when it is out of balance, it can become selfish and may go searching elsewhere for the satisfaction it demands.

Storge, then, stands in contrast to *eros*. It is dispassionate. But it is also devoted. It is quietly loyal. It doesn't require much effort, because it arises naturally, an affection born out of family ties and shared amongst kin. It's about an identity that transcends the self and feels like a given. An inheritance. It is the glue that holds tribes together. It is the kind of love the Hatfields had for one another, and the kind of love the McCoys had for one another, and the kind of love that meant no love was lost between the two families.

Philia takes up residence somewhere between *storge* and *agape*, and if there were an English word for it, that word would be *companionship*. It is about an abiding affection for the other. Yes, it is about loving, but it's just as much about *liking*. Unlike *storge*, which happens spontaneously, *philia* happens *intentionally*. A lot of hard work goes into truly liking someone who is totally different from you. *Philia* is about giving and receiving. It's about *mutual* sacrifice. It is about real-world love, the kind you have to fight for. It's about doing life together until our lives are woven together.

As I stood there in the doorway with my wife, recalling our Gettysburg, I wondered if one of the subtle but fatal flaws in modern marriage is that we keep demanding from it the perfectness of *agape*, when what it has always demanded from us is the tenderness of *philia*. What if God has got *agape* covered and he gave us each other to bring a little more *philia* into the world? It made me think about that breakfast scene in the Bible, sometime shortly after Jesus disappeared from his tomb. It's early morning and the disciples have been fishing. They're catching nothing, when this man they fail to recognize as Jesus shows up on the distant shore and tells them to cast their nets on the other side of the boat. Instantly, their nets are full. This has happened before, and now they recognize the man who gave the order. They return to shore and enjoy a bountiful breakfast together. As the meal is concluding, Jesus asks Peter three times if Peter loves him. The first two times Jesus uses the word *agape*. Peter says yes, but his answer does not satisfy Jesus. The third time Jesus asks the question—the time he is satisfied by Peter's answer—he uses the word *philia*. Am I your *companion*, Peter?

What if marriage specifically—and companionship in general—is asking us to love each other, but it's asking in the language of *philia*?

I was standing there in the doorway, noticing a soccer jersey I thought Quinn had lost months ago, when I began to wonder what it would look like if my wife and I gave our lives to *philia*, to the daily practice of journeying through life alongside each other, witnessing this whole crazy, mysterious, beautiful, sorrowful, messy, terrifying thing together, not as flawless partners but as true companions. Earlier in the day, I'd shared with her my thoughts about *agape* and *philia*. So as we stood there, two traveling companions witnessing together the chaos we are journeying through, I looked at her and asked, "*Philia?*" She looked up at me and smiled.

"Yes," she said, "*philia*."

If you are married and wanting your marriage to heal, or simply wanting to take your marriage to the next level, that level probably isn't *agape*. It's probably *philia*. If you've had difficulty your whole life putting words to why your brother or your sister feels like your best friend, that word probably isn't *storge*. The word is *philia*. If you've spent most of your life in the pursuit of *eros*, and it has always left you hungry for more, the word for the more you are hungering for is probably *philia*. If you're willing to work for it—risk for it, struggle for it, surrender for it—there is a companionship that awaits all of us, in our marriages and families and friendships. *Philia?*

Yes, *philia*.

AND ONE MORE THING ABOUT THIS BOOK

I'd tell all of this to my very brave and somewhat foolish younger self. Then, he'd walk away, into the rest of his day, into the rest of his life. He has just completed his master's thesis on marital conflict. A year from now, he will coauthor a textbook chapter reviewing all the research that has ever been done about marital happiness and unhappiness. Two years after that, he will complete his doctoral dissertation about communication in marriage. Then, a year later, he will graduate, and armed with all this data about relationships, he will begin his career as a couples therapist. However, it will take fourteen more years of life and work and study before he has his most important insight of all:

When it comes to true companionship, all the textbooks in the world are outweighed by a butterfly.

At first, the idea will seem very unscientific to him. However, the more he contemplates it, the more confident he will become about it: the three most poignant stages of a butterfly's life have something essential to teach every aspiring companion about the three most important tasks of true companionship. So, he'll write a book about *philia*, with each part of the book focused on one of these stages and one of these tasks.

Part one, "Grow Quiet: Befriending Your Loneliness," explores the paradoxical prerequisite for true companionship: the ability to be lonely. We tend to resist loneliness, believing it to be a bad thing, but a butterfly *chooses* its loneliness as a *necessary* thing. Early in its life, while still a homely caterpillar, it enters into the solitary interior of a chrysalis to undergo a transformation. We, too, must choose our loneliness as the space in which we are formed into something mature enough for companionship. Lonely things, if they can befriend their loneliness, grow into lovely things. In the quiet, we become.

Part two, "Grow Strong: Embracing Your Struggle," challenges our assumption about the core struggle in every companionship. It is not primarily *between* two people but *within* each person. Every butterfly's life is defined not by a struggle with another butterfly but by a struggle with its own protection. When it is ready to join its companions, it must push its way out of its once protective but now imprisoning chrysalis. It's a challenging struggle, but only through this process does a butterfly strengthen its wings enough to fly. Similarly, in true companionship, we are in an ongoing struggle to push our way out of our own protections. Gradually, in the midst of this struggle, we grow strong enough to love. That's how companionship forms us into flying things.

Part three, "Grow Old: Cherishing Your Time," invites us to cherish that which we often fear: the passage of time and our mortality. The butterfly's life beyond the cocoon usually lasts only a few weeks. Butterflies are lovely things, they are flying things, and they are also dying things. So are we. However, unlike the butterfly, we are the only creatures on the planet who can grieve the loss of life before it happens, so we are the only creatures who can live our lives together as an act of cherishing what will soon be gone. When we bravely accept the end rather than resisting it, we clarify our priorities, sharpen our focus, and love our companions with a little more urgency, while we still have time. Numbered days are cherished days.

"We're all just walking each other home," writes philosopher Ram Dass. For the remainder of these pages, you and I will be walking toward home together, so there are a couple of things you need to know about this leg of the journey. First, each of the three parts of this book begins and ends with a letter to my wife. Second, she's the bravest person I know—brave enough to let me share with you these windows into our companionship. Third, you should probably know her name is Kelly as well. Yes, this is weird and confusing, especially to airport security. So, to eliminate some of the confusion, I've addressed her letters to "M." That is my nickname for her. It stands for "Miracle," because she is my miracle. So much of true companionship—before and after all the hard work—feels like that.

Whether you are single and planning to stay that way, dating and in no rush to be anything else, engaged to the one you've chosen, happily married, angrily fighting, contemplating separation, recovering from divorce, getting remarried, walking through widowhood, confused about how to become a better parent or child or aunt or uncle or sibling or cousin, longing to become a more faithful friend, or waiting upon a friend who can be truly faithful to you, I hope in the singular light of these pages, you will glimpse the great, general light of companionship.

PART 1

GROW QUIET

BEFRIENDING YOUR LONELINESS

I HAVE A WONDERFUL WIFE and three children who, when they are not trying to provoke one another to madness, are the delight of my days. I have friends who would rescue me if I needed rescuing. I have a church where I feel at home. I have therapy clients with whom I share the most personal details of life. I have a speaking career that brings me into the presence of countless lovely souls. I have tens of thousands of fans on Facebook, thousands of followers on Twitter and Instagram, and almost twenty thousand people on my mailing list. I have a device in my pocket that can connect me to all of these people instantaneously. I have a dog who greets me every time I walk in the door as if I am the second coming of Jesus.

And yet, at times, I still feel lonely.

I used to think this meant there was something wrong with me, because I used to think loneliness and brokenness were essentially the same thing—different sides of the same crummy coin. Now I know, our brokenness is about how we were wounded, whereas our loneliness is about how we were *created*. I used to think I was the only one who was lonely. After all, when you look around, other people don't *look* lonely. They just look like they're drinking a latte. So it's easy to assume loneliness is some rare disease you picked up somewhere along the way. Now I know, loneliness isn't a rare thing.

It's a *human* thing.

It is also an essential thing. Like a caterpillar voluntarily retreating into the lonely shell of its chrysalis in order to become what it was meant to be, we too must retreat into our loneliness in order to become who *we* were meant to be. This isn't about enduring our loneliness, or even tolerating it. It's about *choosing* it—befriending it, as one of the most valuable spaces in the human experience. It is in the quiet that our souls grow into the fullness of their beauty, wisdom, and capacity for love.

In the quiet, we are transformed from crawlers into flyers.

A LETTER TO MY WIFE

Before We Belong to Each Other,
I Must First Belong to Myself

Dear M,

Do you remember June 10, 2000?

We'd been dating for about nine months at the time, and it was the weekend of your five-year high school reunion. I stayed behind at Penn State, while you left for a full weekend at the boarding school where you once lived some of your most formative years. You were sleeping in your old dorm, partying late into the night, and of course, reconnecting with your ex-boyfriend of seven years.

I was trying not to feel nauseous all weekend.

I don't remember much about that Saturday, but I do remember the long night. It was hot and humid, and my rented duplex didn't have air conditioning. A small fan pushed soupy air around in the darkness as I lay awake in the small hours of the night, sweating, anxiously wondering what you were doing. Back then, we didn't have cell phones, so I couldn't reach out to you. I just had to lay there and feel it. Finally, about an hour before sunrise, the phone rang. It was you. When I hung up, I sat down at my desk, and I wrote you a poem I called "The Battle Is Won." It was about my struggle with loneliness and self-doubt and insecurity. I dug it up the other day, and it concludes like this:

You will never know
the peace your call brought.
You will never know
how quickly my battle ended.
Your thoughts were with me,
your actions embraced me.
The battle that was waged for nine months,
ended in a twenty-three-minute conversation
    with my friend.
Now, as always,
a part of you is here with me.
But for the first time,
I worry not that a part of me is there with you.

Twenty years later, I'm a little embarrassed for that young man. He is so needy. At the same time, I understand him. The best thing that has ever happened to him is you, and he does not want you to end. He wants to hold on to you with all of his strength. Of course, in doing so, he risks pushing you away. He sort of knows this, but he can't help himself. In this, at least, he is not alone—how often does companionship become a bear hug rather than a gentle embrace, a holding onto rather than a folding into? We don't like to grant much freedom to good things that might leave us.

M, I'm sorry for the times I've held **onto** you, rather than simply holding you.

I'm also a little embarrassed by the finality of the poem. It implies loneliness can be eliminated for good, perhaps even by a single phone call. Time and experience have proven this a naive hope. Now I know, nothing can eliminate my loneliness for good—not even a lifetime of true companionship—because loneliness is part of our humanity, so to become completely unlonely is to become a little inhuman. Having said that, if I could travel back in time, I think I would write a different poem, and I would write it in the dark hours **before** you called. This other poem would be called "Learning to Be Lonely."

> I've been making it up as I go, alone,
> living, searching, in the dark.
> Now, for the first time, my path is illuminated,
> and the light is you.
> I can see my living and my aging and my dying,
>   the whole thing,
> in the glimmer of your presence.
> It makes a young man desperate to keep you near,
>   to keep you alight,
> and, simply, to keep you.
> Can you forgive my desperation,
> while I learn how to be lonely?
> Whether you return to me or not,
> I will make a companion of my very own soul.
> I will stare into the darkness of myself,
> until I find within me enough light to live by.
> Then, knowing I've belonged to myself all along,
> I will be truly free, finally, to belong to you.

M, as I write that, it reminds me of the Buddha. He left his family to meditate under the bodhi tree for forty-nine days, only to discover at the conclusion of those days that enlightenment had been within him all along. Nevertheless, he'd needed to leave to realize he hadn't needed to leave. I suppose marriage is simply one kind of bodhi tree to sit under, as we await the arrival of this kind of enlightenment about loneliness and companionship. There are other trees. There are other places to wait upon the insight that we already belong to ourselves and that on this foundation all true companionship is built. Marriage is my favorite tree, though. Without you, would I have come to trust I could find peace without you? I don't know. The question haunts me.

It is a good haunting.

Love,
F

ABANDONMENT IS NOT LONELINESS

*You are not dead yet, it's not too late
to open your depths by plunging into them
and drink in the life
that reveals itself quietly there.*

RAINER MARIA RILKE

I WAS EIGHT WHEN MY TWO-YEAR-OLD BROTHER fell into the deep end of the pool.

Our family was living in a mobile home at the time. In a way, I think, the whole family was drowning. A couple of years earlier, my parents had both returned to college. My mother had finished her associate's degree, but her meager salary as an entry-level nurse was not enough to keep us in the home we'd been renting while my father finished his bachelor's degree. The trailer park we'd moved into had two perks for a third-grade boy: a huge mountain of dirt to play in and a small community pool to swim in. That was a hard year. My parents were raising three kids while trying to start their lives over. They were tired. All the time. One summer afternoon at the pool, my father's fatigue finally caught up with him.

I'm swimming in the shallow end as I watch my little brother—who cannot swim—toddle over to the pool and walk right off the edge into the deep end. I look around, panicked. We're alone at the pool. No lifeguard. No other families. I'm the only one who has witnessed my brother's aquatic ambition. I shout for my father. Nothing. He has dozed off in a lounge chair, a textbook laying open on his chest. Frantically, I swim toward where my brother went under, plunge downward, and drag him upward. I break the surface with him, and I shout for my father again. Again, nothing. I shout. Nothing. My brother is getting heavier. I don't have the strength to drag him to the pool's edge, nor do I have the strength to keep us both above the waterline at the same time. I do the only thing that comes to mind. I take a deep breath and hoist him upward, the weight of him pushing me downward into the water.

Beneath the surface, it's quiet. I look around, hoping against hope to see another set of legs in the water, but the pool remains empty. I stay under as long as I can, giving my brother as much time to breath as possible, but my own lungs are beginning to burn. So, we switch positions. I break the surface with a great gasp and lose my leverage to keep him above the water. I hold on to him but allow him to drop beneath the surface, as I alternate between filling my lungs with air and emptying them with shouts to my father. Still nothing.

I'm getting scared for my brother, so I take another deep breath, and I switch our positions again. He goes up, and I go down. Nothing has changed beneath the surface. It is still empty. It is still quiet. The sound and fury of what just happened up above is muted down here. I'm not frantically shouting words; I'm steadily treading water. Up there I *felt* alone, but down here I actually *am* alone. Yet, it is somehow more peaceful. A liquid cocoon of sorts.

This is the difference between loneliness and abandonment.

Loneliness is a still and quiet space somewhere beneath the surface of us. Though we may not be alone above the surface, where all the hustle and bustle of life is happening—where all the people are—we *are* all alone on the inside, where no one else can really join us. The center of us is a swimming pool for one. The existence of this lonely space within us does not mean we are broken. It simply means we are human. However, we rarely experience our ordinary loneliness as a mere fact of our humanity, because we rarely experience it *purely*. Usually, our earliest awareness of our loneliness comes bundled up with other things. Things like abandonment.

Abandonment is not a space that exists within us; it's a moment that happens *to* us. It's usually a scary moment. A frantic moment. Whether the abandonment is intentional, like a parent walking out, or completely accidental, like a parent nodding off, it doesn't really matter. Abandonment feels like abandonment, regardless of motivation or cause. The big losses. The painful departures. The small, ordinary moments of neglect. For a child, these moments of abandonment above the water work their tendrils into the tranquility beneath the water. These feelings of abandonment sink into the fact of our loneliness and, without knowing it, we begin to confuse them with each other. They begin to feel like one and the same.

My lungs are burning once more, so my brother and I switch positions again. I breathe, and I shout. Thirty-five years later it's hard to know how many times we went through that cycle of abandonment and loneliness before my father jumped in to save us both. I'm pretty sure, though, the cycle never *really* ended for me. I'm pretty sure it never really ends for many of us. Gasp, shout, quiet submersion, gasp, shout, quiet submersion. It's how we encounter our abandonment. It's how we discover our loneliness. It's how we come to confuse the two.

I'm forty-four years old now, and I've spent the last couple of decades disentangling my experiences of abandonment and loneliness. It's tricky work. There have been more big abandonments along the way. For instance, when my grandfather died during the spring of my freshman year in college, and I never got a chance to say goodbye to him. I felt abandoned, though of course it was no fault of his. Sitting at the desk in my dorm room, having received the news, the telephone back in its cradle, I also felt utterly alone in my grief, because I was. I was the only grandson he ever took golfing every summer morning in those formative years leading up to high school. No one else could know what it felt like to be me losing him. Big abandonment *and* big loneliness. All at once. It makes it hard to disentangle them.

There have been plenty of small abandonments too. Micro-abandonments, if you will. People who would consistently snooze right through my big moments and then want to tell me all about theirs. I've slowly let those folks go. Some abandonment you can't do anything about. Some abandonment you can. However, you will discover, like I have, even as your feelings of abandonment diminish, the fact of your loneliness won't. That's okay, though, because disentangled from your experience of abandonment, your loneliness won't hurt you or scare you the way it once did. It won't feel so much like drowning.

It will feel more like swimming.

The poet Rainer Maria Rilke writes, "It's not too late to open your depths by plunging into them and drink in the life that reveals itself quietly there." I'm starting to learn a new way of relating to my loneliness. It used to feel like my loneliness chose me in the midst of every abandonment; now it feels like I can choose my loneliness in the midst of any moment. These days I go out of my way to grow quiet. I let myself sink beneath the surface of myself, into the depths, where I am totally alone and I can feel my liquid loneliness all around me. I become present to it. Gradually, I'm befriending it.

I hope you too will choose your loneliness over your abandonment. Feelings of abandonment will launch you on a journey of hiding instead of abiding, protection rather than connection, and fighting rather than loving. Loneliness, on the other hand, is in you for a reason. Your loneliness, when you experience it as a friend rather than a foe, will launch you on a mostly peaceful search for connection and closeness and companionship. You don't have to drown in abandonment.

You can learn to swim in your loneliness instead.

NEITHER IS SHAME

*[Man] is not only alone; he also knows
that he is alone. Aware of what he is,
he asks the question of his aloneness.
He asks why he is alone, and how he
can triumph over his being alone.*

PAUL TILLICH

I N 2017, I PUBLISHED A BOOK called *Loveable*. It is a book about the healing of our shame, which is the belief we all pick up somewhere along the way that we are not good enough to be loved as we are, not worthy of companionship, if you will. I wrote the book because I'd spent almost three decades becoming ashamed and almost a full decade becoming more aware of it and more *free* from it. However, following the book's publication, I discovered something a little disconcerting.

Though my shame was shrinking, my loneliness was still lurking.

For a while this confused me. I had been telling myself that shame and loneliness were essentially the same thing, and I assumed as one decreased the other would decrease as well.

Perplexed, I bought a bunch of books about loneliness written by authors I respect, in the hopes of understanding why my shame seemed to be diminishing while my loneliness seemed to be thriving. The reading didn't help. In fact, most of what I read also lumped shame and loneliness together by describing loneliness as an experience which invariably feels shameful. Then, one day, I finally came across the answer I was looking for in a book I already owned. In fact, at the time, I owned almost a hundred of them. The book was *Loveable*.

In it I had written, "Loneliness happens. It is as much a part of life as hunger and sunsets and funerals. It is simply what happens when we grow up and realize we have a universe inside of us to which no other person has access, and that every other person contains an unknowable universe as well." At some deeper level, apparently, I had known all along that, though we tend to lump shame and loneliness together in our minds, they exist separately somewhere at the heart of us. *Loveable* reminded me, once again, loneliness is not an artifact of our woundedness. Loneliness is a *fact* of our *humanness*.

We can have family at home and friends in our neighborhood and followers online and still feel lonely, because loneliness is a constant—even in the midst of a crowd—and *feeling* lonely is merely a *glimpse* of that constant. When you feel lonely for a time, it is your loneliness surfacing and then settling into the depths again. It doesn't mean you're paying a price for something. It simply means you're paying *attention*. So, why do we commonly lump loneliness and shame together, as if they are one and the same? Because we're looking for explanations.

I have a friend who, as an adolescent, told his mother he was going to a friend's house and went to an arcade instead. When he got home, the tokens jingling in his pocket gave him away, and his mother began chasing him around the house with a ruler. My friend had been prepared to get grounded for his deception, but getting hit for the transgression had never crossed his mind. So he dodged and laughed, thinking his mother must be feigning her rage. Out of breath, his mother called his father into the room. My friend expected his father to be more measured. Instead, his father backhanded him across the face. His cheek stung, but the three words inside of his head stung even more.

"It's just me," he thought.

In other words, "What brings me joy brings them rage. What I think warrants punishment to them warrants pain. I'm all by myself. I'm all alone." In the sharp sting of skin on skin, the fact of his loneliness rushed to the surface of him. Like abandonment, abuse has a way of suddenly bringing our attention to this inner reality. Indeed, any experience which reminds us that no one else is seeing the world through our eyes can trigger awareness of our loneliness. However, our minds aren't satisfied with this awareness. Our minds are meaning-making machines. They want an explanation. They want to know *why* we've been abandoned or mistreated or misunderstood. Our minds ask, "*Why* do I feel so lonely?"

Shame is happy to provide the answer.

The voice of shame within us—and perhaps even the voices of shame around us—tells us we are feeling lonely because we *deserve* to be alone. Shame tells us no one can hear us shouting for help because we aren't shouting loudly enough or pleasingly enough or articulately enough, or simply that we aren't worth saving. Shame tells us we got slapped because our sense of justice is wrong or weird or bad. Here's a simple way to expose the difference between your loneliness and your shame. Complete the following sentence: "I feel lonely because . . ." Shame is often everything that comes after the word *because*. Shame is believing your loneliness is a consequence for how badly or strangely you were made.

Shame is weaponized loneliness.

I think back to that eight-year-old boy in the pool, struggling valiantly to keep his brother afloat, and I want to take him under my wing and tell him that his shame has been lying to him all these years. I want to tell him the abandonment he felt that day was not his fault. Indeed, I want to tell him it was *nobody's* fault. I want to tell him that someday he'll be a dad with three kids, and he'll understand exactly how easy it is to fall asleep by the pool. I want to tell him the loneliness he feels beneath the surface isn't his fault either. It's not even a flaw. It's simply a fact.

I want to tell my friend the same thing. I want to tell the teenage boy in him that his abuse and his loneliness are separate things. I want to warn him against letting shame weaponize either one of them. I want to caution him that, over the years, shame will try over and over again to convince him there is something faulty in his laughter and something flawed in his playfulness. I want to reassure him that, though he may feel all alone in his childlike joy, his loneliness is not a punishment. It's just a fact.

And I want to tell you the same thing. You and I, we may never totally get rid of our shame, but we can tell it to keep its hands off our loneliness, thank you very much. Don't let your shame write the story about why your loneliness has surfaced. Try not to add a "because" to any moment in which you become aware of your loneliness. Your shame may pipe up within you, but recognize it for what it is. Don't let it ramble on for too long. Tell it you're not looking for explanations. Tell it you already trust the only real explanation: you are lonely because . . . you are human. Then, your shame will shrink a little more and, finally, you can be a little more alone with your loneliness. It's so much quieter that way.

It's the kind of quiet that can transform you.

3

NOR IS ISOLATION

*We have flown the air like birds
and swum the sea like fishes, but
have yet to learn the simple act of
walking the earth like brothers.*

MARTIN LUTHER KING JR.

I N MIDDLE SCHOOL, OUR OLDEST SON, Aidan, ran on the cross-country team. However, while discussing Aidan's cross-country participation, I would often carelessly refer to it as "track." Cross-country is a sport in which you run several miles off-road, oftentimes on paths through forest or prairie, typically in the autumn. In contrast, track and field happens in the spring, is hosted on a manmade track with manmade obstacles, and consists of a wide array of athletic contests. The first few times I made this mistake Aidan got annoyed, and he would correct me. By the end of middle school, though, my mistake would make him downright angry.

He was angry because I was leaving him extra lonely.

There's an important difference between *ordinary* loneliness—the natural byproduct of a soul traveling around inside of skin

—and the *extra* loneliness that most of us experience from time to time, when it feels like we don't have a true witness to our life. This extra loneliness is better described as *isolation*. Its signature is the haunting sense that no one is *really* paying attention to us, or at least not closely enough to remember the difference between cross-country and track. Loneliness is about the ordinary lonely space *within* us. Isolation is what happens when the space *around* us feels lonely as well.

Once again, it can be difficult to distinguish the two.

Here's the most important distinction. People cannot make us lonely, because we were already lonely when we were made. In the same way that hunger is a craving for food that leads to nourishment, and fatigue is a craving for sleep that leads to restfulness, our loneliness is like a craving for companionship that leads to connectedness. When experienced apart from abandonment and shame and isolation, our ordinary loneliness does not feel like the presence of a bad thing; it feels like a natural instinct for very good things. However, in the same way no one can make you hungry, but they can leave you too hungry by withholding food; and no one can make you fatigued, but they can leave you too exhausted by preventing rest; no one can make you lonely, but they can leave you extra lonely by withholding *philia*.

I love Aidan unconditionally, with an *agape* kind of love, and I hope it is helping him to believe he is loveable and loved. I hope it is easing his sense of shame. However, only *philia* can ease his sense of isolation. You can love someone unconditionally from so far away that you can't tell the difference between track and cross-country, but if you want to love someone *companionably,*

you have to pay close attention. I was loving Aidan unconditionally but not companionably. So I wasn't *making* him lonely,
but I was *leaving* him extra lonely.

During Aidan's freshman year of high school, I got another
chance to attend to him.

For months, I'd been planning and promoting a weekend
retreat for my online community. People were paying for regis-
tration, booking flights and hotels, renting cars. My wife and I
had done the same. The retreat was a little more than two
months away, and everything was coming together nicely. Then,
on a Friday morning, we found out Aidan had been cast as one
of the two leads in his high school musical—as a freshman!
Three days later, on a Monday evening, we got the schedule. His
musical was the same weekend as my retreat.

I felt like I'd been punched in the gut, and I immediately set
about problem solving. I talked to the director, checked flights,
and tinkered with the retreat schedule. I figured out a way to be
at his dress rehearsal, arrive at the retreat in the nick of time, fly
home before dawn on the day of the last show, and hopefully,
assuming no travel delays, get to the high school with minutes
to spare before his final performance.

Then Kelly reminded me about what fuels *philia*. She said the
plan would probably work, but she was going to miss leaning on
the kitchen counter with Aidan—late on opening night, long
after the curtains had dropped—and hearing all about his fear
and his adrenaline and his exhilaration and all of the inner

details of his first high school musical performance. She said we'd be able to ask about those things after it was all said and done, but you can't re-create Friday night on a Sunday afternoon. You have to be there. You have to attend. She was right. I postponed the retreat for six months.

Agape is about perfection, but *philia* is about attention.

When Kelly gave birth to Aidan and I became his father, I also became a spectator. He came with a birth certificate and a ticket for a seat in the front row of his life. Someday, he will probably have a companion who takes my seat. Until then, it's my job to keep it warm. Similarly, when Kelly and I got married, it wasn't just a ceremony; it was a public declaration of my commitment to attend to her. I was volunteering to sit in the front row of *her* life and to not take my eyes off of her. I promised to be a witness to her missed marks and flubbed lines and every note she hits perfectly. I promised to give her a standing ovation when the whole thing is said and done.

Sometimes, though, we forget this.

Sometimes people get distracted and they take their eyes off of us. Sometimes, when we look out at our supposed audience, the seats seem empty altogether. This is what it means to feel isolated, and there are a number of potential reasons for it. Sometimes the auditorium is empty because our people didn't live up to their end of the bargain. Sometimes it's empty because we didn't invite anyone to the show, or because our invitation was too disguised for anyone to recognize. Sometimes the empty auditorium is all in our imagination, a projection of our ordinary loneliness onto the crowd of our witnesses. The circumstances around our isolation can be both frustrating and confusing. If you keep finding this roadblock on your journey toward companionship, it can't hurt to invite someone into the work of removing it from your path—a mentor, a therapist, someone who can guide you as you seek to fill a seat or two in the front row of your life. We're all worthy of at least one set of eyes on us.

On opening night of Aidan's musical, hours after the show concluded, he and one of his castmates came back to our house, still covered in makeup and the thrill of their first performance. As we sat there with them—leaning on the island in the middle of the kitchen, the bulb above us like a spotlight in the otherwise dark house, asking them questions, enjoying their stories about what went right and what went wrong and what it felt like to live the whole night—I knew Kelly was right. You can't recreate Friday night on a Sunday afternoon. You have to be there, in the front row, paying attention.

That's what it means to be a true companion.

Having said that, try to remember, even the best witnesses will not be able to witness the quiet and lonely place at the center of you. Though I showed up with *philia* on Aidan's big night, there is a big space within him I can never witness. He will carry that space around within him his entire life, into and through every companionship, and it will not go away. His extra loneliness will be eased, but his ordinary loneliness will go on. So will yours. That's okay.

It will keep you on the journey, traveling ever deeper into true companionship.

4

A CAUTIONARY NOTE ABOUT THE DIGITAL CROWD

*To turn from everything to one face is to
find oneself face to face with everything.*

ELIZABETH BOWEN

S EVERAL MONTHS AGO, our daughter, Caitlin, and I were
standing in the toy section of our local bookstore when she
picked up a Magic 8-Ball from the shelf, shook it, and waited
for her answer to float to the surface of the inky liquid. When
the word *Yes* appeared in the window, she wiped her brow in a
grand gesture of great relief. I asked her what she had asked the
8-Ball. Her answer took my breath away.

"Will I ever feel like I fit in this world?"

I think the Magic 8-Ball gave Caitlin the right answer. Now
more than ever, she probably *will* feel like she fits in this world,
because we live in an age of digital miracles. We can connect to
billions of people with a few taps of a finger or swipes of a thumb.

Just one generation ago, you could only be in one place at a time. In your whole life, you'd meet maybe a few thousand people. Now, the whole world congregates in the palm of your hand. So, Caitlin probably will cross digital paths with enough people who are enough like her to feel like she fits in this world. However, this will give rise to an even more troubling question. Why, if I feel like I fit with so many, do I still feel so alone?

Around 2012, something happened to teenagers in the United States. For two consecutive decades, their reported levels of happiness had been increasing, and suddenly the trend reversed direction. At the same time, rates of reported loneliness and depression spiked, with a 50 percent increase in teenagers hospitalized for suicidal thoughts between 2008 and 2015. This kind of sudden decline in teen mental health has happened before, but always in connection to a major cultural upheaval or a cataclysmic global event. So, what was the most significant cultural revolution of 2012?

For the first time, more Americans owned a smartphone than did not.

Around the same time, social media became the go-to method for congregating and communicating among adolescents. Digital connection quickly began replacing analog companionship. Given a choice between a driver's license and a smartphone, many kids suddenly preferred a phone. After all, a car can only drive you to one place to see a handful of people, but a phone can transport you everywhere to see *everyone*. Caitlin's generation will be the most digitally connected generation in human history. Yet they may end up utterly isolated in the analog world.

Of course, I don't believe these technologies have created our loneliness. Rather, I think we have created these technologies *out* of our loneliness. In an attempt to fix our ordinary loneliness, we gathered a digital crowd, but the digital crowd is leaving us more isolated than ever. This is confusing to us, because when we maintain a bunch of Snapchat streaks we feel momentarily accepted—like we really fit in this world, as Caitlin would say. So it seems like our loneliness should be shrinking, but instead it remains what it is and what it will always be, while our sense of isolation slowly grows alongside it. Then, we return to the bottomless well of digital connection, hoping this time it will finally satisfy our thirst for companionship.

It will not.

The morning after Caitlin asked her question of the Magic 8-Ball, I made her chocolate chip pancakes. As I mixed them, it occurred to me that digital connection is like chocolate chips in the pancake recipe of life. It is tasty and tempting to consume by the bagful. It feels good momentarily, and it goes down relatively easily. In contrast, analog companionship is more like the eggs. It holds everything together. It has cracks in it, and it's messy, and if you don't cook it all the way through it can even make you sick. However, without it, the recipe of life just doesn't work very well.

The digital crowd brings with it the thrill of discovering you fit *in* from a distance, whereas analog companionship brings with it the challenge of figuring out how to fit *together*, up close and personal. Analog companionship has flesh and blood in its code, not 1s and 0s. It has salt in its tears, not pixels. There's a big difference between a digital thumbs-up and a warm hug.

Nevertheless, because the digital crowd momentarily obliterates our sense of isolation, we are giving more and more of our relational energy to it, rather than to analog companionship. In other words, we keep reaching for the chocolate chips, but we need to be cracking a few eggs instead.

The day after I made pancakes for Caitlin was Father's Day, and I began the day by kayaking alone down my favorite river in north central Illinois. For long stretches of river, there is no sign of civilization at all, and you can float for miles without encountering another human being. Furthermore, there is no cellphone reception, so you are as alone as you'll ever be in a world where the digital crowd is always knocking at your virtual door, one push notification at a time. I enjoyed being alone for about ten minutes. By the first bend in the river, though, my isolation wasn't sitting well.

Out of habit, I reached for my phone. No signal. I waved it in the air like we do now, hoping for bars. Nothing. I put the expensive brick back in its watertight compartment. My feelings of isolation, however, were not so easy to compartmentalize. I had an urge to check my social media accounts. I let the urge float by. I had an urge to text a friend I hadn't talked to in a long time. I let it float by. My mind wandered ahead to the upcoming week, and I wanted to check my calendar. I let the desire float by. I left my digital crowd upstream. I paddled. I looked around.

I took it all in.

The wind in the treetops. The sun on fire. When my loneliness surfaced, instead of reaching for my phone, I reached over the boat. I grazed the surface of the analog river with my analog hand. I attended to all of these tangible realities: wind and sun and water. These *elements*. It made me think of how, in my faith tradition, we receive two elements every Sunday: bread and wine. They are meant to symbolize the flesh and blood of Jesus. It's a weekly reminder that uploading prayers to supernatural gods can only take us so far, that flesh-and-blood presence is the kind of analog companionship we all really need.

Flesh and blood.

On that Father's Day morning, my restless urge to reach out to the digital crowd never really left me. But in the midst of it I became aware of myself floating toward the flesh-and-blood, analog companionship in my own life. It would be waiting for me on the dock at the end of my journey. Kelly and our three kids. Waving. Chattering. Fighting. Smelling of sunscreen and sweat, of flesh and blood, of bath water and river water, of baptism by life. I had not immersed myself in the rushing waters of the digital crowd, so I had time to value the flow of this analog companionship in my life, this sometimes joyous, sometimes painful, always challenging, elemental *philia*.

Analog companionship can be hard. It can't rescue you from all your isolation, because it can't be there for every bend in the river. Nor can it eliminate your ordinary loneliness, because it can't see all the way inside of you. However, if you are not cultivating analog companionship on a daily basis—the day-to-day exchange of care and chaos and connection—your sense of isolation will grow more quickly than your Instagram following ever could. On the other hand, if you commit to the practice of companionship—if you turn from everything to one face, as the novelist Elizabeth Bowen says—then when you arrive at the dock at the end of your journey, you might just discover yourself face to face with everything you could ask for. You might just discover this Magic 8-Ball we call life has given you the answer you'd been hoping for all along.

And we analog companions,
wipe our holy human brows
in a grand gesture
of great relief.

5

YOU ARE A GREAT AND PRECIOUS THING

All great and precious things are lonely.

JOHN STEINBECK

W HAT IS LONELINESS?
Abandonment is painful, but it is not loneliness. Abandonment is unheard shouting above the surface of our lives, while loneliness is a quiet place beneath the surface of *ourselves*, and it is a constant, regardless of who comes and goes. Likewise, shame is painful, but it is not loneliness. Shame is one of the more hurtful *explanations* for the unchanging reality of our loneliness, but when it dissipates, our loneliness persists. Similarly, isolation can be quite painful, but it is not loneliness. Isolation can be reduced by the attentive presence of someone in the front row of our analog life, but ordinary loneliness cannot be reduced by a crowd of any size. So, what *is* loneliness, exactly?

Loneliness is something you can see in a brick wall, an animated movie, and a super moon.

I'm sitting in a sushi restaurant at noon on a Wednesday, waiting for Kelly. I make the conscious decision to keep the digital crowd in my pocket, and I stare at the exposed brick wall in front of me instead. My eyes wander slowly upward, and I see something a little disconcerting. One stretch of wall is not flat. In fact, it's wavy. As far as I can tell, it does not seem to have buckled over time. It looks strong and sturdy. Rather, it appears that almost a century ago the bricks in this section of the wall were simply laid a little less uniformly than usual. It was made this way. I'm guessing nowhere in the cosmos is there another brick wall exactly like it.

In those bricks, I see myself, and you, and all of us.

Each of us shares more than 99.9 percent of our DNA with everyone else. And yet there are about three million differences between your genome and any other human being's. Three million ways in which you are idiosyncratic and odd, different and weird, wavy instead of flat. Three million ways in which you are totally unique. This kind of uniqueness is not about snowflakes that melt in the heat. This is about bricks *formed* by heat into a particular kind of strength that no one else shares. This is about three million microcosmic ways in which no one else can really relate to the way you were made. To who you are. To your *self*.

Not to mention your *story*. The sum total of your uniqueness can be calculated by multiplying the three million ways in which your self is unique by the countless ways your story is unique. What you get is too many digits to comprehend. I look at that wall and I see you and me, at first glance looking a lot like every other human being, but also in places wavy and rippling and imperfect and perfectly unique. This is no accident. Your bricks were laid in a way that no one else's bricks were laid. This doesn't make you broken, it makes you *you*. This is a lovely thing. But it is also a very hard thing, because of this:

Our loneliness is the shadow side of our uniqueness.

Writing often makes me anxious because I like things orderly and predictable, but the creative process is messy and uncertain. For instance, at the outset of any writing project, you think you know what you want to say, but as you start writing, you can see it's changing into something unexpected. Once again, the whole thing will be a mystery you'll solve as you go. Furthermore, someone may even be *paying* you to solve it. What were they *thinking*?

In the midst of such creative panic, it helps me to immerse myself in the stories of other creatives who are also wading through the mess of making something. Once, I found a video by a successful recording artist, revealing the months of painstaking trial and error it took to finish one of his most popular songs. Suddenly, I felt a little less alone in my creative quandaries. I sent the video to Kelly, telling her how amazing it was. I didn't hear anything back. Later, I asked if she had watched it. Her response? "I got through a minute of it, but, meh, I'm not sure what you liked about it." And just like that, boom. Loneliness.

For years, I confused moments of loneliness like this in my marriage with abandonment, shame, or isolation, and I would fire the first salvo in yet another marital battle. These days, though, I'm a little quicker to distinguish my loneliness from my wounds, and it has made all the difference in our companionship. The truth is, I didn't feel abandoned by her reaction to the video—she wasn't going anywhere. It wasn't shame—she never implied I wasn't good enough. And it wasn't isolation—she was right there with me, in the analog world. It was just loneliness, even with this woman who rearranged her work schedule to meet me for sushi in the middle of a Wednesday. This woman who has bent over backward to support my writing career, embraced more about who I am than any other person I've known, and shared half of my life story with me. This woman who has been my companion through so much thick and so much thin. Right there next to her in our kitchen, I felt lonely. Why? Because I will always be a little alone within the experience of being me. This is not a fault of hers. Nor is it a glitch in creation. It's simply a *part* of creation. She can't possibly comprehend those three million unique genetic variations in the way I'm made. The fact of our loneliness exists as the shadow side of this uniqueness.

Three days a week, I work and write from home. Nine months of the year, this arrangement works well. Summertime with the kids home is a different story, however, and summertime with a writing deadline is a *very* different story. The day after I met

Kelly at that sushi restaurant, the kids' social calendar was feeling like a big barrier between me and a project I was trying to finish, and my creative anxiety was starting to feel a little more like creative terror. I was sitting at my computer, trying to put together a paragraph like this one, when nine-year-old Caitlin walked into my office. I was expecting an interruption, but she gave me inspiration instead. She put her hand on my shoulder and said four words: "I believe in you."

Those four words felt like *philia*. They were a way of saying, "I can't possibly comprehend three million ways in which you are different from me, but I can have faith in the parts of you I can't understand." The apostle Paul writes that "faith is confidence in what we hope for and assurance about what we do not see." In a way, I guess, companionship is too.

Sure, it shrinks our loneliness when someone can truly understand something about who we are and what we're experiencing. In fact, as a psychologist, that's a big part of my job. Somehow, though, having someone *bet* on us can be even more comforting than having someone *get* us. Our loneliness warms to this kind of grace.

A day later, on a Friday afternoon, while Aidan and I are driving somewhere together, I ask him what it feels like when he goes beneath the surface of himself and experiences his loneliness. He looks sideways at me like I've got a screw loose and responds, "I don't get into my head long enough to feel lonely." I drop the subject. Then, a day later, on Saturday morning, I announce that our family is going to the theater at noon to see the latest animated family flick. Suddenly, Aidan starts acting like a real jerk, criticizing the movie and everyone planning to go to it. To his credit, he catches himself mid-bluster. I ask him why he went on the attack. He thinks for a moment and then admits, "I guess I feel like a loser because I'm actually looking forward to going to a kids' movie in the middle of a Saturday. None of my friends would do that."

I tell him that's not called being a loser; it's called being *lonely*.

Among his friends, he's unique in this way. His uniqueness is part of what makes him a great and precious thing. That's a fact. However, the shadow side of that fact is his loneliness. I tell him I'm impressed he let himself feel it instead of staying outside of himself and trying to avoid it. I encourage him to keep doing so. I tell him the only way to get more familiar with the best and most valuable parts of himself is to get closer to his loneliness as well. I tell him it can be disconcerting at first, but it's worth it in the end.

Finally, a day later, on a Sunday morning, Quinn shows me a light within a light.

I'm rinsing the breakfast dishes, focused on my task, when he comes up behind me and points out the window in front of me. The dawn is just breaking, and hanging above the trees across the road is a brilliantly bright orb. It is a super moon, meaning the moon is as close as it can get to Earth on the night it also happens to be full, making it as large and as beautiful as it can possibly be. As we gaze at the super moon, I imagine the other side of it—the side of it in deep, deep shadow.

The dark side of the super moon.

What if it's true? What if your uniqueness makes you a super moon worthy of awe and wonder, and your loneliness is simply the shadow side of your uniqueness? What if your loneliness is the inevitable counterpart to everything that is great and precious and most beautiful about you? Might that change the way you relate to your loneliness? Would you quit rejecting or running from the loneliest parts of you? Would you be more likely to welcome your loneliness, not as a dark omen about who you are, but as an opportunity to learn more about the best parts of who you can become?

I think that's how this human thing is supposed to work: we walk the barren landscape of our loneliness, mapping its terrain, the craters and the dust, seeking its liminal edge, until one day we glimpse a bright horizon, light from Somewhere bending around the curvature of our self, this great and precious thing we've been all along. This super moon like none other.

6

SO LEARN HOW TO BE ALONE

The necessary thing is after all but this:
solitude, great inner solitude. Going-
into-oneself and for hours meeting no
one—this one must be able to attain.

RAINER MARIA RILKE

K ELLY AND I USED TO HAVE slightly different approaches to late-night conflict: I liked to fight and she liked to sleep. While I would demand to work it out, she'd roll over and pass out. I'd lie awake next to her, trying to remain calm, though every once in a while I'd go a little nuts. One time, I flipped the bedroom light on and off, on and off, on and off, until she was forced to wake up and talk it out. There's a *slight* chance that happened more than once.

Over time, though, I had to admit that when I was able to let it go for the night, the conversation almost always went better in the morning. It turns out rested people are more reasonable people. Slowly, I began to appreciate that she was caring for herself first so she'd have the energy to care for me better. Nevertheless, many a night, I felt terribly alone lying awake in that quiet bed, with her breathing peacefully beside me. It went on that way for a decade or so, until one cold winter night that changed my life. Finally, I went on my hero's journey.

In 1949, professor of literature Joseph Campbell published a book called *The Hero with a Thousand Faces*. It identified a pattern found in the stories of every culture across time and place. He called it "the hero's journey," and it has become the template for all meaningful storytelling. Whenever you take your kids to a satisfying Pixar movie, you are watching the stages of the hero's journey. On the other hand, if you conclude a book or a Netflix binge feeling vaguely underwhelmed, it's probably because the story did not honor the stages of the hero's journey. Learning how to be truly alone is a hero's journey too.

RESISTING OUR LONELINESS

The first stage of the hero's journey is *the ordinary world*. Here, the hero is living a relatively normal life, mostly oblivious to the adventure that awaits. In the ordinary world, loneliness lies dormant in our depths. For me, that life-changing night a number of years ago began like any other. Kelly and I were planning to attend a large public event, and we knew a small, private gathering of friends would be happening first. I assumed we would be invited. We left home unaware that the night would not go as expected.

The hero's ordinary world is then disrupted by *the call to adventure*. The call to adventure into our loneliness can happen anywhere, anytime. You might be on a leisurely walk on a late summer evening, when your attention is drawn to an empty playground in the distance, and you notice a solitary swing rocking back and forth ever so slightly in some imperceptible breeze, and something about that swing swaying in the gloaming rouses the loneliness at the center of you. The subtlest of things may call you: a forlorn pair of shoes tied together and draped over a telephone line in the dull buzzing light of a street lamp, a crumbling stone wall running straight away through some forgotten field, a single rivulet of water running down a windowpane on a rainy day, densely populated cities or lightly traveled highways, ringing in your ears no one else can hear, feelings in your heart no one else can feel.

My call to adventure unfolded slowly over the course of the evening, as it gradually dawned on me that we had not been invited. For a while, I told myself everyone was just running late. Gradually, though, it occurred to me they may already be gathering without us. The idea of it gave me a mild case of emotional indigestion. Then, as the public event was about to get underway, I got confirmation the private gathering had already happened. My emotional indigestion turned into emotional vertigo. From the depths of me, my loneliness was calling.

Plagued by uncertainty, self-doubt, and fear, the hero always *refuses the call*. At first, we tend to refuse the call into our loneliness as well. Instead of listening to it, we reach for our devices and their digital distractions. We pour a gin and tonic. We sleep with somebody. We find a new obsession. We work harder at our jobs. We fight harder and try harder in our relationships. Parents over-parent and lovers over-love. Whatever your preferred method, every refusal amounts to the same thing: we go outward so we don't have to go inward.

Later that evening I lay awake in bed for hours, searching for a comforting explanation, engaging in my favorite refusal of the call: problem solving. Of course, problem solving can be very useful, and it is a strength of mine. However, sometimes I use it to analyze what's going on *around* me, rather than attending to what's going on *within* me. So, over and over again, I dissected a list of potentially reassuring explanations, all the while ignoring the call of my loneliness.

Then, in every hero's journey—including the journey into our loneliness—*the hero meets a mentor* who nudges the hero into their adventure. Your loneliness mentor might be the voice of a therapist or a trusted friend or family member. It might be the voice of an author on the page of a book you're reading. It might be a voice arising from within you, somehow a part of you but also wiser than you. My mentor had the voice of a child.

It was well past midnight and my problem solving was mostly exhausted, when I heard within me a youthful voice saying something exceptionally difficult to hear. It spoke a truth I'd been trying to ignore for a very long time, and the first part of it took my breath away. "They are more important to you than you are to them." Nudge, nudge. The second part of the truth took my past away and handed it back to me, irreversibly rearranged. "That's how it's always been." Push, *push*.

And with that, my ordinary world was no more.

MOVING TOWARD OUR LONELINESS

The hero's refusal gives way to resolve as they *cross the threshold* from the ordinary world into the extraordinary world. This is the moment in which we actually begin the inward journey toward and into our three million unique variations. I crossed the threshold as a series of memories crashed in. Over the years, I'd done my best to write them off as isolated incidents: trips taken with me left behind, for instance, or arrivals celebrated with me not included. However, taken seriously and taken together, they told a painful truth. For most of my life, these friends had been tops on my guest list, but oftentimes I didn't even show up on theirs. I was optional to them.

"Who are you?" I asked that small, childlike voice within me.

"I am you," he said.

"How old are you?" I asked again.

"I'm ten," he responded.

"What do I do?" I asked him a third time. His answer surprised me.

"Let's go for a ride," he suggested.

So we did.

My invisible mentor and I pulled out of the driveway at two o'clock in the morning. We drove out of town and into the flat, frozen darkness of an Illinois winter. It was quiet in the car. I looked through the windshield and upward into the cold cosmos. One star appeared to twinkle harder than all the rest. In combination with the events of the evening, that solitary star almost undid me. I felt so much extra loneliness I could barely stand to stay in my own skin. I wanted to drink. I wanted to distract. I wanted to do anything but experience what I was experiencing.

This, too, is part of the hero's journey.

After crossing the threshold into the extraordinary world, the hero is always *tested by foes and assisted by allies*. As we cross the threshold on the inward journey toward our loneliness, aban-donment, shame, and isolation will rear their ugly heads. You will feel the fullness of every moment you've ever been left behind. You will feel the self-rejection of every inadequacy you've ever ascribed to yourself. The despair about every va-cancy in your story will swell and crescendo. Your extra lone-liness will become almost unbearable. Consequently, your resis-tance will rise up once again, and the urge to distract yourself from your inner world will grow stronger than ever.

When that happens, instead of reaching for a device, scan the horizon for an ally. If you do so, some help *will* arrive. Your allies may come to you in the form of a book club or a yoga class or a church small group or a meditation sangha or a prayer group or a therapist or a friend or a sibling or a spouse. None of these allies will take *away* your loneliness; they will simply walk with you *toward* it. Driving through the darkness on that cold winter night, the ally who came to my aid was my most cherished spir-itual guide, author Henri Nouwen. I recalled his words in a book I once read, and they were the encouragement I needed to stay the course:

> As hard as it is to believe that the dry desolate desert can yield endless varieties of flowers, it is equally hard to imagine that our loneliness is hiding unknown beauty. The movement from loneliness to solitude, however, is the beginning of any spiritual life because it is the movement from the restless senses to the restful spirit, from the outward-reaching cravings to the inward-reaching search, from the fearful clinging to the fearless play.

With the help of allies like that, the hero continues on and finally arrives at *the inmost cave*, a moment of reckoning in which the hero faces the truth of their past, solidifies their identity, and gets a glimpse of what must come next. You and I (if we persist on our journey toward our loneliness) will eventually arrive at our inmost cave—the place within us where no companion has ever, can ever, nor will ever dwell along with us. Here, we face the very ordinary, simply human, always inevitable thread of loneliness that runs throughout our story. We see with greater clarity the three million ways in which no one can be expected to understand us—the three million ways in which we are totally unique and thus uniquely valuable.

On the backroads of a bitingly cold Illinois night, my invisible mentor spoke up for the first time in a while. His voice had a husky sadness to it, but his words rang true. "I think you chose those friends because they were good friends. They made you feel very unalone for a very long time. You assumed they'd make you feel that way forever, but," and here his voice cracked with emotion, "I guess that's not really their job." In my inmost cave, I was shown the truth: while they were the people who eased my isolation for a while, I was not the person who eased theirs. They had other people for that. There wasn't anything to be angry about, nor anything to forgive; there was simply a new kind of friendship to pursue. It was time to stop longing for old friends and time to start befriending a new one: my loneliness.

It was time to finally befriend *myself*.

The hero emerges from the inmost cave with a *reward*, and this reward sees the hero through the rest of their journey. When the inmost cave is our loneliness, our reward is the transformation wrought by our solitude: a sense of wholeness, an unparalleled presence, self-acceptance of our uniqueness, and true acceptance of the otherness of others. Suddenly, alive within you is the greatest reward of all: the capacity to be truly alone. You have a newfound sense of strength and resilience. You know you've got what it takes. You've got *yourself*.

In the otherwise inky darkness, I passed a farmstead where the dim light over a kitchen sink revealed an old, lonesome farmhouse. An hour earlier, the sight of it would have triggered an excruciating sense of isolation, and I would have resisted it, probably by searching for better music on my phone. Now, though, having befriended my loneliness, it brought instead a peace that surpassed all understanding.

It was a lonely light, and so was I, and all was well with my soul.

RETURNING FROM OUR LONELINESS

Having secured their reward, the hero begins the journey home. However, the road home is not an easy one, because the bad guys always rally, even more ferociously than before. As a result, the hero always faces an *all-is-lost moment* in which it appears all progress will be erased and the foes will finally win.

My foes rallied around three o'clock. I had just turned in the direction of home when all my self-doubt returned. I got embarrassed about going on a bizarre road trip with my ten-year-old self. I chided myself for being so touchy-feely. I told myself the whole journey had been hogwash. I worried about what I should do the next time I saw my friends. I considered kicking my invisible mentor out of the car so I could go back to problem solving. For a moment, it felt like all might be lost.

However, every hero's journey culminates in a *resurrection moment*, a final moment of redemption with far-reaching ramifications for the hero and everyone back in the ordinary world. In other words, rather than being defeated by our abandonment, shame, and isolation, we draw upon the rewards of our solitude, and the hardest parts of our story suddenly lose their power to distort our loneliness into something broken.

Instead of dismissing my mentor, I called on his wisdom once again. I asked him what to do next, and he told me to take the next left. A few minutes later, we pulled up to the curb in front of the school I had attended when I was his age. He pointed at a tall streetlamp illuminating a parking lot to the side of the school building.

Then, a new memory surfaced.

It's another wintery day, long ago. Dusk is descending. I'm ten years old and I've walked from my home back to the school grounds, for a reason long forgotten. There's just enough light left in the afternoon sky so that when I turn my eyes upward, I can see huge snowflakes falling, dark against the platinum background of the clouds above. Snow gradually accumulates on my nose and eyelashes. I rest this way for a while.

The world around me is muffled by the newly fallen snow. Slowly, I open my mouth and begin to capture snowflakes on my tongue. I'm completely alone, and I'm in love with the moment. For a while on a cold, dim, lonely afternoon in my youth, I befriend my loneliness. I feel the rewards of solitude, and it is all I need to stay warm.

"That is how you do it," said my mentor, drawing me back to the present. "In the same way your wife"—he blushed slightly as he said the word *wife*—"takes care of herself first so she can take better care of you later, you take care of yourself first. I think you call this self-care, but it's mostly just paying attention to me and asking me what I'm needing and even, from time to time, what I'm *wanting*."

"Does a good beer after a long day count as good self-care?" I asked him.

"Ugh," he said, pretending to stick his finger down his throat. "Gag me with a spoon."

Then, he was gone.

LOVING FROM OUR LONELINESS

Every cycle of the hero's journey concludes with the hero returning to the place from which they set forth, bringing with them *a gift for their people*. Several months after my late-night drive, winter was giving way to springtime, and along with it came the liturgical season of Lent, a season in which the death of Jesus is observed through the sacrifice of various pleasures or luxuries. I decided to make my Lenten practice a gift for Kelly, too, by giving up my demands for her to take care of my loneliness.

For Lent, I decided to practice *self*-care.

And over the course of forty days something new began to happen. The ordinary, repetitive activities of daily living—those we mindlessly rush through, like brushing our teeth, doing the laundry, or washing the dishes—were transformed. I stopped experiencing them as barriers to well-being and instead began experiencing them as deeply meaningful acts of self-care. Also, I noticed when I was clenching my jaw and cared for myself by relaxing it. A deep breath became a way to nurture myself. I sipped my coffee slowly, and I chose not to pour a second cup, because I'm too dependent on the stimulant. I ate a salad instead of a pizza, to nourish myself. For dessert, I ate a handful of chocolate chips, instead of a bagful. I asked my younger self what he wanted to do the most. He reminded me of long-ago walks through his grandparents' forest. So, I went for walks, and I paid attention to sunlight on pine needles, the metallic scent of winter becoming springtime, birds calling in the treetops. By Easter, most of my restlessness was being transformed into restfulness—my fearful clinging into fearless play.

In the midst of bedtime conflict with Kelly, the urge to flip our bedroom light on and off, on and off, on and off, dissipated. Instead, I remembered one star that twinkled brighter than all the rest, a dim light over the kitchen sink of a solitary farmstead, and the fading gray light on a winter afternoon several decades ago. I remembered my hero's journey, and I stopped resisting my loneliness for good. I befriended it once and for all. I reaped the rewards of solitude: I was able to be alone and to leave Kelly alone. It was a gift to her, but it was a gift to me too.

Then, next to her, I slept.

7

MAYBE EVEN
FIND GOD IN IT

Are you looking for me?
I am in the next seat.
My shoulder is against yours.

KABIR

I HAVE HAD A LONG and complicated relationship with God. I don't remember the early years of my life when, I suspect, God felt as close to me as my breath. Few of us do. Memories tend to begin later. My memories of God begin in a church. It was a small church that made God seem small, and it was a scared church that made God seem scary. Of course, as a kid, I did not understand the God I was being given was shaped like the insecurity of those giving him to me. I just assumed God was less loving and less mysterious than almost everyone I knew.

Then, two decades later, things got blessedly complicated.

After years of praying from Sunday morning pews for the divine to fully show up in my life, a bigger God did finally show up. It *was* a Sunday morning, but it was not in a church. It happened in a hotel lobby on a Marine Corps base in Virginia, where my sister-in-law had gotten married the day before. It was Father's Day, and I'd awoken in the predawn hours embroiled in the same resentment I'd harbored for most of my marriage. I was angry at Kelly for not giving me more attention the day before, and I was angry because I figured Father's Day would be more of the same.

However, for the first time in my life, rather than stewing in my anger, I did something different. I listened for a better voice within me—the ancient voice of God, the voice I call grace—a voice I'd heard *about* but never actually heard *myself*. On that morning, for the first time, I heard the voice of grace within me, and it was whispering of my worthiness. It assured me that I was loveable, regardless of how much attention I was getting from Kelly. In almost an instant, my resentment was replaced by contentment, and I peacefully left the room for the hotel lobby, where I planned to continue listening. At that hour, I thought I'd be alone in the lobby.

Instead, I met three people who changed my life and my faith forever.

The first was the desk clerk, a stout woman on her hands and knees, sweating, cleaning up vomit left by drunken hotel guests just hours before. I'd come to the lobby to be with God, expecting to do so by praying quietly. So, I was tempted to leave her alone to her work. Then, for the second time that morning, the voice of grace spoke up within me. It said, "If I am in you, then I am in her. Being with her *is* being with me. You came here to pray. Helping her *is* praying." I offered to help. She politely declined. Her eyes were grateful anyway.

I found a nearby chair, sat down, and closed my eyes, beginning to pray like I'd been taught in that tiny church so many years before. Still a little oblivious to what was happening that morning, I asked God to show up for real. As soon as I did so, the lobby door opened, and a moaning young woman entered. The desk clerk lumbered to her feet, took the woman's arm, and helped her shuffle toward the elevator. Again, the voice of grace whispered within me, saying, "Sometimes you'll find me in prayer and sometimes you'll find me in pain. Sometimes they are the same thing." I got up, too, and took the ailing woman's other arm. After the elevator doors closed, the desk clerk told me the woman was returning from the hospital. The evening before her husband had forced her to load their moving truck by herself. Hours later, she had miscarried their first child.

If God was within me, God was within her, and thus within her tragedy.

The divine was growing bigger by the moment, but old habits are hard to break, so I once again returned to my chair and my intention to pray as I'd been taught. I closed my eyes. I asked God to show up again. I waited. At first, I heard nothing. Then, someone spoke to me. I opened my eyes. Sitting in front of me was a young boy with the biggest and bluest eyes I've ever seen. I asked him his name. He told me. Then, he told me that his father had recently been killed in combat. For the first time, he was fatherless on Father's Day.

My old habits broke for good.

I knew if the divine was within me it was also within this boy. Finally, I knew what the apostle Paul meant when he talked about praying ceaselessly: talking to this boy *was* prayer. Finally,

I knew the God within us is bigger and better than the God up in the sky—the tiny God I'd been taught about as a child—could ever be. Henri Nouwen writes, "It is in the midst of the chaotic suffering of humanity that the Holy Spirit, the Spirit of Love, makes himself visible. But can we recognize his presence?" At her retreats, author and speaker Paula D'Arcy has been known to say the same thing in another way: "God comes to us disguised as our life."

God comes to us disguised as a desk clerk mopping up vomit and a hemorrhaging young mother in grief and a fatherless child on Father's Day morning. This idea is not new. Indeed, it is found in much of our religion and poetry. For instance, in the Old Testament, after a night spent wrestling with God in his dreams, Jacob wakes to declare, "Surely, the LORD is in this place, and I was not aware of it." God comes to us disguised as our struggling places.

In the New Testament, this God arrives as our human companion and, from an ancient hillside, tells us we will not find him where we are looking. We expect to find him in reward, happiness, power, righteousness, justice, perfection, victory, and status. However, Jesus teaches that God can *actually* be found in more ordinary things like poverty, grief, humility, hunger, mercy, longing, surrender, and persecution. God comes to us disguised as small and suffering things.

The poet Elizabeth Barrett Browning put it this way:

Earth's crammed with heaven,
And every common bush afire with God,
But only he who sees takes off his shoes;
The rest sit round and pluck blackberries.

God comes to us disguised as every common bush. Jesus tried to tell us this, and he called it the good news. He told us the kingdom of heaven is at hand. He said the kingdom of heaven is near. The church I grew up in tried to shrink his teaching down. They said "near" meant "just about to happen." Two thousand years have cast reasonable doubt on that interpretation. On a Sunday morning in a hotel lobby, I came to appreciate a bigger and better interpretation of those words. The kingdom of heaven is right *now*. God is *here*. Earth is crammed with the divine in disguise. I tell you all of this because, after several years of journeying into my loneliness, I've found God disguised in a very surprising place: my inmost cave. God also comes to us disguised as our loneliness.

Loneliness is God at first glance.

This might seem improbable to you at first. It did to me. The disguises of God always do. Sweating desk clerks. Grieving mothers. Fatherless children. Our struggles. Our suffering. Our shrubbery. Our *life*. However, this truth about loneliness is a little less disguised in the person of Jesus. What I mean is, every time we find him running into God, it's not in crowded places. It's in quiet places. A transfiguration with just a few onlookers on a remote mountaintop. An intimate conversation on the Mount of Olives while everyone else slept. And of course, the ultimate reunion, on the loneliest of crosses. I think it's possible we're still waiting on God after two thousand years because we are missing him right here, right now, disguised as our quietest place: our loneliness. I can't give you proof of this. I can only give you permission.

I give you permission to quit waiting and start *journeying*.

Notice the call within you. Catch yourself refusing it. Let this book and these words be your mentor, nudging you across the threshold into your extraordinary inner world. Set aside spaces for space. Block out time for becoming. Turn off your phone and grow truly quiet. Breathe. Breathe again. Breathe a thousand times, until some of the noise around you and some of the foes within you begin to subside. This probably won't happen immediately. It usually takes time and practice—days, months, maybe even years. Welcome the allies who may join you along the way, until one day you come at long last upon that cave within you. Enter into the solitude of it, reap the rewards it has to offer you, and bring the gift of it back to all of us. Then, *do it again*, until the path becomes so well-worn you know it by heart—until your loneliness begins to feel like a friend itself.

Welcome it. Converse with it. Get to know it. Embrace it. Then, eventually, on some distant day, you might pull back from an embrace with your loneliness to discover you are looking into *more* than your loneliness. You are looking into a great mystery. You might realize that, until now, you had only been seeing the surface of your loneliness, it's most comprehensible parts. Now, though, you see it has always harbored something *else*, a great secret: loneliness is merely an alias it uses when it visits this thing called space and time. In every other realm, in every other place where souls are unleashed from skin, it goes by a different name. That name is *holiness*.

Loneliness is merely the first taste of holiness.

Then, perhaps, your whole life will flash before your eyes again. You might recall all of those lonely moments—the swaying swing, the forlorn sneakers, the crumbling stone wall, the rivulet of rain—and you might realize that if you had stared into those moments for just a little longer, truly befriending them instead of resisting them, you would have seen the holiness embedded in all the loneliness. Theologian Paul Tillich put it this way: "In these moments of solitude something is done to us. The center of our being, the innermost self that is the ground of our aloneness, is elevated to the divine center and taken into it. Therein can we rest without losing ourselves."

God does not come alongside us *in* our loneliness, but *as* our loneliness. God redeemed loneliness from the very beginning not by eliminating it but by *becoming* it. Our loneliness, in the end, is both the force drawing us back to the divine, and the divine itself. Perhaps this is the narrow way Jesus spoke of, and the reason few choose to walk it. In the ancient words of Jacob, surely God was in this place and we weren't even aware of it. He is in the next seat, disguised as your loneliness.

His shoulder is against yours.

8

AND LET SOMEONE STAND WITH YOU FOR A WHILE

*It's like singing on a boat during a terrible storm
at sea. You can't stop the raging storm, but
singing can change the hearts and spirits of the
people who are together on that ship.*

ANNE LAMOTT

T HE FIRST DAY OF FOURTH GRADE was one of the loneliest of my life. Our family had just moved away from that
trailer park in the hills of Missouri back to the small town in
Illinois where I was born. I was returning to a school I'd left
behind three years earlier. First graders had grown into fourth
graders. Some of the faces were vaguely familiar. Most were not.
It seemed no one recognized me. I had no companion.

So, upon arriving at school, I asked my mom to stand with
me until the bell rang. Back then, asking your mom to stand
with you on the fourth-grade playground could easily result in a

333

nasty nickname that would follow you all the way through high school. I decided the risk was worth it, because the possibility of future rejection I could handle, but the presence of my loneliness I could not. Of course, at the time, I did not really know any of this. I just knew I wanted someone to stand with me on the playground for a little while. I wanted her to abide with me.

I'm sure I didn't know that word *abide* back then. It's a lovely word. It means to remain with, to continue with, to stay with, to dwell with, to stand with, to endure with, to wait with. With, with, with. When someone abides with you, it means they are choosing to be with you, before all others. It implies that they will stay with you through whatever comes, that they will sing with you on this boat called companionship during the terrible storms raging on the sea of life. Abiding doesn't stop the storm, but it changes the hearts and spirits of those who choose to sail together.

I was a quiet boy. My mother is a quiet woman. Thank goodness abiding doesn't always require singing together. Sometimes it's as simple as standing together. I can't remember if any words passed between us that morning. If they did, I don't remember what they were. Nevertheless, she agreed to remain with me. She chose to abide. She stood with me on the playground for a little while.

In 2018, Britain created the Ministry of Loneliness. Its stated goal is to address the epidemic of loneliness in the modern world and to alleviate its public health consequences. Britain estimates approximately nine million of its citizens are often or always feeling lonely. They speculate it costs employers in the United Kingdom approximately $3.5 billion annually. And it's not just Britain. The US Surgeon General recently proclaimed that the health effects of loneliness are equivalent to smoking approximately fifteen cigarettes per day. Joe Camel has been replaced by Joe Lonely.

However, I wonder if, in part, those health effects are related to the ways we are defining loneliness and companionship in relationship to one another. For instance, in an April 2018 *TIME* magazine article about the newly appointed British Minister of Loneliness, loneliness is defined as "the feeling of lacking or losing companionship." The implication here is that companionship is the given of being human and, when it is lost, loneliness is the natural consequence, like a punishment for failed relationships. Ironically, this definition of loneliness creates more shame about being alone—more *weaponized* loneliness—and thus more reason to hide ourselves away from each other. If it were up to me, I'd rename the whole thing. I'd get specific: the British Ministry of Abandonment, Shame, and Isolation.

Then, we could stop treating loneliness like a terminal disease. Instead of defining loneliness as the feeling of lacking companionship, we could turn the definition on its head and define *companionship* as the feeling of lacking isolation, healing abandonment, and diminishing shame. Then, we could talk about how loneliness and companionship actually come together. In true companionship, loneliness doesn't diminish entirely. Our three million unique genes remain as unique as ever. No matter how close we get, we can't get close enough to live on the inside of anyone else. So, true companionship is not a space in which our loneliness is eliminated. True companionship is a space in which our loneliness is *shared*.

On the first day of fourth grade I felt lonely, and on the first day of *seventeenth* grade I still felt lonely. It was August 1999. I'd recently broken up with my high school sweetheart of almost four years, had graduated from the University of Illinois a few months earlier, and was about to begin my doctoral program at Penn State. I loaded all of my worldly possessions into my car and my parents' minivan, and we set out in a caravan for the hills of central Pennsylvania. My parents got me settled. Then, I asked them to linger in town for a day or two. In other words, at the age of twenty-two, I asked my mom to stand with me on the playground for just a little while longer.

Of course, they couldn't abide forever. So, a few days later, there I was once again, at a new school full of unfamiliar faces, alone. I met Kelly the next day. She'd broken up with her high school sweetheart of seven years that morning, and we met for the first time that afternoon. I know how that must look: two lonely souls, running from their loneliness by running into the arms of each other. There's probably some truth to it, actually. Dating is what happens when you look around the playground of your life and ask someone to stand with you for a little while. Marriage is what happens when you ask them to stand with you for a *long* while.

Yet, I stand by most of the reasons I became enthralled with Kelly: her painful story and her fierce resilience, her tender heart and her adventurous spirit, the joy in her laugh and the fire in her eyes, and the way she can make any forlorn soul feel like the most important person in the world. So, I asked her to stand with me on the playground for a little while, and for a little while, it felt like my loneliness had disappeared almost completely. Is it any wonder the early days of a romance are so intoxicating? I figured she would eventually make my loneliness go away altogether and, with that confidence, I asked her to marry me. In hindsight, I realize I was asking the impossible.

When we get married, we often believe we are leaving our loneliness behind us, at the wedding altar. We aren't. Getting married doesn't eliminate loneliness, it *multiplies* it. Whereas previously you were traveling through life with only your own loneliness, now you are traveling with your loneliness *and* the loneliness of your companion. Marriage doesn't end loneliness; it *doubles* it. You end up with a total of six million ways you can't comprehend each other.

Marriage is a double date with the shadow sides of our uniqueness.

I wish I'd known all this when I asked Kelly to stand with me on the playground for the rest of our days. I wish I'd known loneliness was already standing there on the playground with me. I wish I'd known what I know now: true companionship is about allowing our loneliness to stand between us, not as something that divides us but as something that *unites* us. It's not about blaming our loneliness on each other; it's about sharing our loneliness *with* each other. It's not about thinking of our loneliness as dangerous ground, but about embracing our mutual loneliness as our most *common* ground. After all, I may not understand what it's like to be Kelly, but I can understand what it's like to be *lonely*.

A LETTER TO MY WIFE

You Are My Destination

Dear M,

I remember our friend's words.

We'd driven cross-country from Chicago to Boston with the sole purpose of celebrating New Year's Eve with her family. She was reflecting on our companionship with them, when she said, "It feels really good that you drove all this way just to see us." In other words, it feels really good to be someone's destination. We all want to be on the receiving end of someone's GPS coordinates, to be the place at which someone else is longing to arrive. We all want someone's heart to be oriented toward us first, before all others. M, her words made me realize how much my relationship to you has changed over the years. I used to think of you as my savior.

Now you are, simply, my destination.

The savior years were not easy ones for you, I know. In those days, I saw loneliness as my enemy. I wanted it defeated and destroyed, and I thought you would be my conquering hero. When we got married, I said I was giving my heart to you. That is sort of silly. Two decades later, my heart is still very much in my own chest. However, I realize now, I did give you my loneliness, and I expected you to do something to it. That expectation might have ended our travels together. Fortunately, I gradually accepted how companionship really works.

It's not a place where our loneliness is removed; it's a place where our loneliness is **revealed**.

Now I know my loneliness will be with me forever, and that is not a problem. Indeed, it has been an **opportunity**. It has been a chance to reveal a vulnerable part of myself to you, and it has been a chance to hear about your loneliness in return. A chance for both of us to learn we are not the only ones feeling alone in the crowd. Over time, instead of becoming free **from** loneliness, I have become free **for** loneliness. Free to touch it without despair, to share it without fear, and to befriend it without shame.

In other words, free to make you my destination instead of my savior.

Exactly four years before we met, I arrived as a freshman at the University of Illinois. I'd visited the sprawling campus several times during the previous year because a friend was already attending there. When I visited, I always went straight to her dormitory, which was at the center of campus in a building called the Newman Center. From there, we'd visit various destinations on campus, like the student union or the bookstore. By the time I arrived on campus as a freshman, the best way I knew to get around, no matter my destination, was to go to the Newman Center first, and then walk from there.

M, I no longer think of my heart as something I've given to you. I think of it as the Newman Center of my self. The place I go first to orient me to all other things. The place where I encounter my loneliness and my humanity and my divinity, including my arrogance and anger, my fear and frustration, my sorrow and shame, my joy and peace, and interwoven with all of that, my capacity to love. Then, having oriented myself there, I set out for my destination. When I forget to do this, I inevitably get lost, so I try to remember it well these days. And of course, there are many destinations on this campus I call my life: our kids and our friends, my clients and my readers, my writing and my speaking.

But, I want you to know, you are always my first stop, my first choice.

Recently, I arrived home on a Friday morning after a community meeting, with lots of email to return and lots of writing to do. Some Fridays you are still home when I return from this meeting. Some weeks you are not. I was not thinking about you when I pulled into the driveway. I was thinking about my to-do list. Nevertheless, when the garage door went up and that old minivan of ours was not in the garage, I suddenly felt a tinge of sadness. Apparently, even when I'm not thinking about you, my heart is oriented toward you.

You have truly become my destination.

Our family lives well beyond city lights now, so the moon shines brightly, and you can see manmade satellites traversing the night sky. From here, both the moon and the satellites can look a little lonely. The truth is, though, they both have been given something to orbit around, and there is loveliness in that kind of loneliness. In true companionship, we learn how to orbit around something **without becoming that thing**. So, here's a vow better than any I made to you on our wedding day: I'm your Man in the Moon. I will always gaze upon you. For as long as I exist, you will be my first choice.

You will always be my destination.

Love,

F

PART 2

GROW STRONG

EMBRACING
YOUR STRUGGLE

W E COME INTO THE WORLD with a true self, created for us and gifted to us, and it is absolutely worthy of love and belonging.

However, at some point, usually very early in life, we experience shame, which is the message communicated through words and silence, through action and inaction, by friends and family, by peers and pastors, that we are not good enough to be loved the way we are. Consequently, as children, we all do the wise thing and begin to build a false self in order to protect us from more shame while earning us the love we so deeply desire. Our false self is constructed like a castle, with walls to hide us, cannons to defend us, and thrones to elevate us. Like any castle, though, our false self also has a drawbridge— a point of vulnerability—through which our true self can exit so we can love and be loved authentically.

A couple of years ago, I was keynoting a men's retreat, and I told all of this to the guys in attendance. As I described the drawbridge, the group leader remarked humorously that, when you leave your false self behind, your true self gets to go running naked through the countryside. We all laughed and had fun with the concept. However, after returning from the retreat, the idea nagged at me, because companionship rarely *feels* that way, does it?

Rather, true companionship feels much more like an in-between place in which we are increasingly embodying our true self, while *also* struggling to free ourselves from our false self. In other words, the true-self-versus-false-self duality ignores most of the most important loving going on in our lives. Those of us who have chosen to enter into the preciousness and peril of *philia* are much more likely to be inhabiting a *third* self, neither true nor false but some amalgam of both—a struggling self, a transitioning self, a becoming self—our *emerging* self. As a butterfly emerges from its cocoon, its wings grow strong enough to finally fly.

Likewise, in this struggle with our false self, our hearts grow strong enough to truly love.

A LETTER TO MY WIFE

Love Goes the Long Way

Dear M,

With six hushed words from the back seat, Caitlin took my breath away.

We were on that road trip last spring break, when you suggested making a detour to show the kids your old boarding school. You wanted them to get a taste of your youth, to approach this special place of yours for the very first time on the very same road you used to travel. However, as we got closer, we realized we were arriving at the school on the wrong road and from the wrong direction. To correct our error, we would have to drive all the way back through town, adding fifteen minutes to a detour that had already significantly delayed our travels.

You were crestfallen.

I pride myself on my productivity and efficiency, so, usually, when something you want takes longer than expected, I grumble about having to be flexible. On that day, though, I was practically Gumby. I told you if it would make you happy we would do it, no matter how much time it took. You gratefully reached out and took my hand. Then, Caitlin asked her question from the back seat:

"Will my husband be like that?"

M, I never told you why I was too choked up to answer her.

Caitlin assumes we love each other, so she also assumes that what we **do** to each other is what love does. In other words, if we are in constant competition with each other, she will learn love battles. If we are unfaithful to each other, she will learn love wanders. If we have some invisible gulf between us, she will learn love avoids. So, I was too choked up to speak because Caitlin had just learned a good lesson about love.

Love goes the long way.

Love will sacrifice what it can for the joy of another. Of course, I can't **make** you happy. Some days there's a fire in your eyes and there's nothing I can do to put it out. Joy is an inside job. You are responsible for finding it within you. However, I do believe I can increase the **odds** of your happiness. In other words, I want our marriage to give you as many reasons as possible to smile.

I want to go the long way for you.

The question is, if I **want** to go the long way for you, why do I so often complain about it? As a man named Paul once said, why do I do the things I do not want to do, and why do I not do the things I do want to do? I think it has to do with the thin, nearly translucent layer of protection I still wear around me. Most people can't even see it anymore. Nevertheless, within the close confines of our companionship, you and I both bump up against it all the time.

It's my ambition.

For most of my life, I have used my ability to achieve and accomplish as a layer of protection against a world that I fear will reject me. In everything I do there is this drive to be the best—to be on the top so I don't have to feel like I'm on the outside.

However, there is nothing triumphant in going backward to correct one of your mistakes. That is merely love going the long way. You have given me ample opportunity to bump up against this protection of mine and, like a butterfly trying to free itself from its protective chrysalis, I'm trying to push my way out of it, so I can fly the long way with you.

M, you weren't there a few weeks later, when Caitlin asked another question from the back seat.

We were beginning our weekly round of carpool, and she asked if we could pick up her friends in the opposite of our usual order. She said it would be quicker. I told her I didn't think so. In fact, Mr. Ambitious goes the way he goes because he thinks it's most efficient. However, I told her we could try her way and then compare them. As we approached the second friend's house, Caitlin declared this new way had been faster. I voiced my disagreement. Over my shoulder, I heard an exasperated sigh. "What's wrong?" I asked. Her words were tinged with the same wistfulness as her sigh.

"We have different tastes today."

M, her words made me think of us. On any given day, we have different tastes. We have differences of opinion, conflicting preferences, diverging goals, incompatible beliefs, and intertwined with all of that inevitable stuff is our protective stuff. You and I have the same taste in coffee, but we rarely get through our morning cup before we encounter our different tastes about **something**. We're learning to live authentically with these differences between us, while leaving our protections behind us.

This hasn't happened overnight.

It's been a long, loving struggle.

With that in mind, Mr. Ambitious looked in the rearview mirror, smiled, and told Caitlin we could travel this new route from now on. She looked thoughtful for a moment, smiled back at me, and then suggested we alternate routes for the rest of the year. In a grade-school carpool, your husband and daughter **both** *went the long way. Then, two months later, Caitlin made me that Father's Day card that read, simply, "Happy Father's Day! I am myself and you are too and I like it that way. I really love you." I can't think of a better way to describe the graceful reward of this great, sacred struggle that is true companionship: I am myself and you are too, and I like it that way.*

M, I hope **that** *is what Caitlin is learning from watching our marriage. I hope she is learning love goes the long way. I hope she is learning that, in true companionship, the long way is the long, slow sacrifice of our protections. I hope she's witnessing us mutually committed to leaving our cocoons behind.*

I hope she's watching as two people take flight together.

Love,

F

9

OBSERVE YOUR PROTECTIONS

*In the beginning I was so young and such
a stranger to myself I hardly existed. I had
to go out into the world and see it and hear it
and react to it, before I knew at all who I
was, what I was, what I wanted to be.*

MARY OLIVER

I'M GRATEFUL I MET HIM BEFORE HE RETIRED.

At the time, I was completing my doctoral degree at a veterans' hospital in the suburbs of Chicago. I'd mostly enjoyed my training there, but I was beginning to feel frustrated with almost every client. My supervisor at the time was a wise senior psychologist, just a few years from retirement. One day, I walked into his office and exclaimed, "All of my clients are stuck!" He turned in his chair to look at me. A smile played at the corners of his mouth. Then he said something that has, over the years, saved almost every relationship in my life, both personally and professionally.

"When you are stuck with a client, it's because you don't have the same goals."

At first, it seemed too simple. Then I began testing it out, and he was right. When I asked my clients directly, I discovered their goals were entirely different from mine. For instance, sometimes I was wanting to help them feel happy, while they were just needing to feel their grief. Or I was trying to save their marriage, while they were trying to exit it. Every time, once we clarified and agreed on our goals, our relationship and the therapy thrived.

It's true of every kind of companionship. If you and your companions feel mired in anything from staleness to combativeness, it's probably because you don't share the same goals. This wisdom can be invaluable on a day-to-day level as we figure out how to do life together. However, my supervisor's wisdom is even more essential as you shift your attention from *what* you are fighting about on a daily basis to *how* you are fighting about it over time.

We all need to agree our goal is to fight like butterflies.

The fight of a butterfly's life is not against another butterfly but against its own protection. When a caterpillar first spins its cocoon, the cocoon is a thick and opaque exoskeleton, like armor within which it can safely undergo its metamorphosis. However, by the time the butterfly is ready to emerge, the protective chrysalis has become a thin and nearly invisible prison. The butterfly can't see it. The butterfly can only sense it when it bumps up against it. Then the butterfly pushes back on what it cannot see, until the old protection finally gives way. To our detriment, we human companions resist the central tenets of this struggle in three significant ways.

We often fail to perceive our own protections. There are several reasons for this. First, in the beginning we wielded our protections clumsily, so they were easily noticeable. Over time, however, we become skilled at using them to stay safe. Our protections become habits, and habits are hard to notice. They don't feel like a choice; they feel like a given. Second, our protections were originally necessary. They preserved us as we were growing up, so it's easy to overlook the moment when they tip from help into hindrance. Finally, our protections are often woven from the gossamer thread of our worthiest traits, so it can be difficult to perceive them as problematic. My ambition, for instance, produces a lot of good things, so it's not easy to admit that it can become too much of a good thing. For these reasons, we often remain unaware of our protections, even as we try to love right through them.

So, instead, we focus on our companion's cocoon. It's easier to see someone else's protections, so we take it upon ourselves to tell the ones we love about the thoughts, feelings, and behaviors that are protecting and imprisoning them. This is almost always a waste of time. Unless we have been invited to give such feedback, it is unlikely to penetrate the cocoons of the ones we love. Furthermore, it is quite likely that if we are giving unsolicited feedback about the protections of another, the feedback itself may be one of *our* protections. It's easier to push blame onto the cocoons of everyone else than to push our way out of our own chrysalis.

Then, we try to free our companion from their protections. This usually breaks bad too. First of all, we are totally unequipped, from within our own cocoon, to free another human being from their protection. We lack the freedom of movement to do so. We lack the grace that comes through our own struggle. Furthermore, even if we could free the ones we love, it would be crippling to them. A butterfly cut from its cocoon prematurely will never fly. It is a loving thing to allow the ones we love their own strengthening struggle. As Jesus once said, it's better to focus on the plank in our own eye than the sliver in our companion's.

True companionship must be the mutual agreement to make the observation of our *own* protections the goal of our days.

Can you recall your long-ago moments of chrysalis spinning?

I can remember an afternoon in childhood at a family reunion. At the time, I was terribly self-conscious of the baby fat accumulating on my preadolescent body, and a distant cousin poured a bucket of cold water over me in front of everyone. My wet T-shirt clung to my pudgy frame, exposing my insecure flesh to the entire crowd. Wrapped in a towel and drenched by humiliation, I vowed never to be seen like that again. So I spun ways of hiding from everyone.

I remember the time, about a year later, when an older boy on the elementary school playground slid a metal bat between my legs and lifted. I remember the excruciating pain in my groin and in my heart. Right then and there, I decided I would never leave myself that defenseless ever again. If my body wasn't big enough to protect me, then something else would have to be. So, I spun ways of fighting back with my words.

I remember a couple of years later, on the middle school playground, when the words of the other boys cut me like a knife—words claiming my boyhood didn't measure up, me with my gentle way of being and my sentimental way of feeling. I remember how vulnerable I felt to all of it, with no words of my own sharp enough to wound them in return. So, I spun ways of rising above all of them.

For decades, my protections grew thicker and thicker, and they were all anyone could see of me. In Mary Oliver's words, it seemed like my original self barely existed anymore. Most of us live in this state for many years, divided into our protections and the part of us we are protecting. False self and true self. Protective self and connective self. We remain in this state of suspended animation until something triggers our emergence. Franciscan theologian Richard Rohr suggests the trigger is usually either great love or great suffering, or both. For me, the trigger was a person. The trigger was Kelly.

I was so determined to love her well that I was willing to do crazy things to make it possible. Nutty things, like pushing my way out of my defensive cocoon into the light of day. Insane things, like trying to leave my treasured protections in order to cultivate true connection. Wacky things, like trying to take flight as the person I was made to embody from the very beginning. For twenty years, I have been trying to exit my false self, so I can truly give my true self to her.

I didn't know it would take this long to emerge.

I remember one of the first times I really observed my emerging self. I had volunteered to coach Quinn's first-grade soccer team. Before the first weekend of games, the park district had sent an email reminder to all coaches with one phrase in all capital letters: WE ARE ONE TEAM WITH ONE GOAL. Of course, the goal they were referring to was youth development: teamwork, sportsmanship, physical fitness, and good-natured fun. But why the reminder? And why all caps?

Several days later, I found out.

At that age, both teams run around in a big cluster, chasing the undersized soccer ball. If it weren't for the differently colored shirts, you'd think they *were* one team. The whole thing looks aimless and silly. However, the parents on the sidelines were not acting aimless and silly. They shouted at their children intensely, lamented ferociously, and cheered madly when a goal was scored. The rules of the league mandated no official scorekeeping, but you could see the scoreboards in the eyes of every parent. I scoffed at how ridiculous they were all acting.

Then, I saw my emerging self.

I observed what had been going on within me, and I realized I'd been keeping score too—until we got down by double digits. Then I'd quit counting and started focusing on how we were all one team with one goal. How convenient. In a single moment of awareness, I glimpsed within me my true self, which wants to see every kid have some fun, and my false self, which wants to see *my* kid get a win. I saw the part of me that knows people are more important than points, and the part of me that acts like points are way more important than people. I observed my true self, struggling to emerge through all my ambition.

94

You, too, can learn to observe your emerging self by becoming more familiar with your protections. In the following pages, we will focus on nine of them. Likely, one or two of them will stand out to you as your go-to methods for protection. However, if you pay close attention to your emergence, you may ultimately see some of each in your chrysalis. Also, as you struggle out of your protections, you'll be tempted to hope for a great epiphany and an instantaneous exodus from them. Try not to rush it, though. It takes time to grow strong enough to fly. Just remember, you and your companions are one team with one goal: to embrace the struggle.

10

ANGER

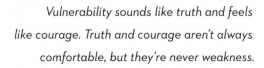

Vulnerability sounds like truth and feels
like courage. Truth and courage aren't always
comfortable, but they're never weakness.

BRENÉ BROWN

T HE FIRST TIME THE PHONE RINGS, I ignore it. I'm
under a writing deadline and trying to stay focused. When it
rings a minute later, I glance at it. It's Aidan's high school calling.
The first call was from the school as well. Something uncom-
fortable swells somewhere in my chest, but I ignore it and continue typing. A minute later, it rings again. The thing in my chest
swells bigger this time. I pick up the phone. It's the school nurse.

Aidan had been hit by a car while biking to school.

The feeling in my chest bursts open into full-blown fear. I ask
if he is all right, and she asks if I'd like to talk with him. Aidan
gets on the phone. He tells me he is mostly all right. The nurse
thinks an ankle and a rib might be broken, but it could have
been worse. Then, he makes a joke. "I'm so glad I wasn't wearing

a helmet, Dad, because I'm not sure what happened when I flew over the hood, but my hair looks great right now."

Some switch within me flips. The anxious feeling in my chest immediately disappears and something far safer and more comfortable swells in my head, right behind my eyes. It's anger. I'm angry he wasn't wearing a helmet, and I'm angry he had to ride a bike in the first place, because he had been too disorganized to catch his carpool on time. Suddenly, I'm terse and businesslike, commanding him to be waiting for me at the curb when I arrive to pick him up. I'm sure the emotional about-face is confusing to him, but for the moment, I don't really care. Also, it's not *actually* confusing. Aidan's life had been threatened. Anxiety and anger are two opposing reactions to the very same threat. And they cannot coexist.

This is something you learn in introductory psychology, but it ought to be taught to all of us on the first day of a mandatory class on relationships. When we are threatened, our bodies instantly enter a state of arousal designed to help us react quickly and efficiently to the threat. Then, by instinct, we act upon that arousal in one of two ways: fight or flight. Anger or anxiety. Aggression or evacuation. You cannot fight and flee at the same time. They are two mutually exclusive commitments. However, there is something you *can* do.

You can learn to *choose* your response, rather than letting it choose you.

I once had a friend who was plagued by panic attacks. He'd tried everything to get them under control—therapy, meditation, medication. Nothing worked. Then, one day his therapist suggested the next time he felt a panic attack coming on,

97

he should make himself angry instead. She told him to focus on the injustices in his past and in the world that most enrage him. A week later, he was in a crowd and noticed his anxiety increasing. He did what she had told him, and within a minute or two he was as angry as can be. And his anxiety was gone. If my friend can dispel his fear by choosing his anger, then you and I can do it the other way around too. We can dispel our anger by choosing our fear.

I hang up the phone with Aidan and try to calm myself. As I do so, I look out the window and see on the outside a massive spider that has been living there for about a week. The spider is round with babies. Every day, it splays out its legs with their bright, menacing stripes, making itself look as intimidating as possible. The truth is, it's as vulnerable as a creature can be. A toddler could squash it between its fingertips. The spider's show of strength is protecting so much fragility. It can't possibly flee, so it acts like it wants to fight. In that spider, I see the way I work and the way a lot of companionship works.

We don't want to flee, so we pretend we want to fight.

It brings to mind something that happened to me several months earlier while leading a couples retreat with a cofacilitator. She was conducting an exercise with the participants, and I decided to play along. First, she said, "When you are in the middle of intense conflict with your beloved, where do you feel it in your body? Write it down." I wrote, *My chest*. Next, she asked us to visualize that emotion in our body and to write a one-sentence description of it. I surprised myself when I wrote, *It is a ball of white-hot anxiety in the center of my chest.* When I fight with Kelly, I may look angry and aggressive on the outside. However, on the inside, I'm feeling afraid and vulnerable.

My cofacilitator continued by asking us to imagine a door on that emotion. She encouraged us to open the door and to enter that space within us. Once we could picture ourselves inside of it, she suggested that a smaller, younger version of ourselves was huddled in the corner of that space. She told us to write down the age of that child. I wrote down the number eight. Then, she encouraged us to invite the younger version of us into conversation, including two specific questions. First, I asked little me what he needed from me. He said, immediately, "I just need a safe space to feel my fear, because I don't think the adults around me can handle it." Second, at her direction, I asked him for his even higher and nobler longing. He told me, "I want to forgive the people who could not be that safe space for me." He wanted to let go of his anger.

Now, standing in my bathroom, I want to let go of my anger all over again.

As I get in the car, I get a little help in letting go. A song is playing on the radio, and one particular lyric stands out: "It might be over soon . . . all these years . . . it might be over soon." I let myself fully feel the day. I choose to fully feel my fear again. My son could have been killed today. The baby boy I used to rock on my lap while trading goofy faces, he was very close to not being here anymore. Any day, really, it might be over soon. Last week, I found a new brown spot on my abdomen. It might be over soon. The woman I love more than anything in the world could walk out at any moment. I don't think she will, but she could. It might be over soon. The vulnerability of it all is sometimes almost too much to bear. It's so tempting to flip the switch and act aggressively instead. It's so tempting to display our stripes and prepare for a fight.

I'm pulling up to the high school when a couple who approached me after a session at another couples retreat. They were about to go to lunch, and they were concerned their lunch conversation would devolve into anger once again, as it had so frequently over the past year. They wanted to have a different kind of conversation, and they wanted my advice. I reminded them of the teaching that says "perfect love drives out fear," but I told them perfect love doesn't drive out fear by *eliminating* fear; it drives out fear by *expressing* it.

The confession of our fears to each other may be the highest form of *philia*.

So, I'd told them there was one way they could guarantee a different conversation at lunch: don't speak unless you are discussing your fears. In other words, I'd told them to stop protecting through shows of angry strength, and to start connecting through the practice of *true* strength, which is the confession of our fragility. Author Madeleine L'Engle writes, "When we were children, we used to think that when we were grown-up we would no longer be vulnerable. But to grow up is to accept vulnerability." To be alive is to be vulnerable. And to be a true companion is to silence your anger by talking about your fear.

Aidan was standing on the curb when I pulled up to the high school. He got in the car, and I chose to trade my anger for my anxiety. I told him his accident had scared me. He admitted it had scared him too. We hugged. I joked that God sure had gone out of his way to create extra study time for his upcoming Spanish test. He replied, "Tú estás cierto," with more than a little uncertainty. We laughed.

The doctor eventually ordered x-rays. They came back negative. Aidan's bones and hopes and dreams were all still unbroken. My fears could be put to rest for another day. But just for a day—because every day brings with it new threats, new reasons to be aroused. Every day brings with it new opportunities to choose our fear over our anger. New chances to trade our big, bad stripes for a little loving vulnerability. It might be over soon. We can get angry about that, or we can get honest about it. We can trade our fight for our fragility.

It may not feel comfortable, but it will feel like companionship.

11

PEACEFAKING

For Jesus, peace seems to have meant not the
absence of struggle but the presence of love.

FREDERICK BUECHNER

O N A FOURTH OF JULY MORNING, I'm trying to be a peacemaker but succeeding only at peace*faking*. Just three weeks earlier, Kelly completed her first half Ironman triathlon. She's in the best shape of her life. I'm in the best shape of my adult life, too, which is to say, I can bend over to pick up a LEGO I've just stepped on without worrying too much about throwing out my back. My limit for a bike ride is about fifteen miles. In her triathlon, Kelly cycled fifty-six miles right after a mile-long swim and right before a thirteen-mile run. She can literally ride laps around me.

We are starting our holiday with a bike ride together and, as we approach mile ten of a fourteen-mile loop, she suggests we turn around and go home the way we came. I do the math. It would add an extra six miles to our trip and would be, by far, my longest ride of the year. I hesitate to answer. We stop. She prods me. I continue to hesitate, and while doing so, I notice there's a quiet, cautionary voice whispering within me. I shush it, because I want to increase the odds of Kelly's happiness.

After all, love goes the long way, right?

So, we turn around and begin the ten-mile ride home. The steep hill we had just raced down is now the steep hill we must climb up. I'm giving it everything I've got, and she's beginning to pull ahead of me. I give more. I notice that voice whispering a little louder within me. I shush it again. I pedal harder. I'm keeping up with her, but the cost is high. I'm experiencing sensations in my legs that do not bode well.

Then, finally, the whisper breaks through. "Kelly, you *will* keep up with her. You will rise to the challenge. That's what you do. But you are going to have to use up everything within you to do so, and this day is just getting started. You plan to stand for two hours while the kids paint Main Street this morning, three more hours at a carnival this afternoon, and at least two more hours at a concert tonight. You need to pace yourself today, and this is the opposite of pacing yourself."

It's the voice of my true self. It is made to get out and fly, but on this Independence Day morning I have kept it imprisoned within the cocoon of my false self. This peacemaking instinct that I thought was connecting me to my wife was really a *peace-faking* instinct that was protecting me from disagreement with her, or at least her disappointment in me. Really, I had not *made* peace. I had faked it. At the cost of my truest self.

Without realizing it, most of us define peace as the absence of conflict. So, when we mute our most authentic voice in order to avoid disagreement, we believe we have made peace. Churches seem particularly susceptible to this misconception. For instance, I was recently reprimanded by a client's pastor for encouraging my client to speak up in her marriage. The pastor told me the goal of counseling should be to make peace in the marriage, not sow division. Many Christian communities, it seems, have adopted a definition of peace that requires them to keep their mouths shut, no matter what.

Ironically, Jesus did anything *but* keep his mouth shut. He was cheeky with his parents at the age of twelve after they forgot him in a temple. He talked back to his mother when she asked him to do everyone a big favor at a wedding. When the religious authorities demanded answers from him, he responded instead with questions of his own. He publicly accused those same authorities of being hypocrites, over and over again. He responded to church abuses by fashioning a whip and turning over tables. He was called the Prince of Peace, but he seems to be a walking, preaching, whipping contradiction. He's not.

He was simply guided by a different definition of peace.

Coming from the Jewish tradition, he would have been more intimately familiar with the Hebrew word for peace, which is *shalom*. *Shalom* does not mean the absence of conflict; it means the presence of wholeness, of unity, of togetherness. Jesus knew peacefaking actually *prevented* the sacred struggle of real peacemaking. He did not seek conflict, but he did honor his most whole and holy self, and he embraced whatever conflict might come along with it.

As Kelly and I are approaching the top of the hill, I remember the evening before.

The kids and I had met her at our favorite restaurant. After dinner, I asked Caitlin what music she would like to play on the way home. She hesitated. I prodded her. She hesitated again. Then, unlike her old man, she listened to the whisper within her and told me what it was saying, "Dad, I want to ride home with Momma tonight. I love you, too, and I'll ride with you next time, but tonight I want to go with her." Yes, this stung a little. I felt a little rejected. Yet that feeling was dwarfed by my delight in Caitlin's clarity of self.

What would Jesus do? He wouldn't try to fake peace by suppressing his own voice and giving everybody exactly what they wanted. On the other hand, he also wouldn't speak truth with no regard for its impact on others. That's just another form of protection. Rather, he would give voice to his true self while honoring the true self of everyone around him. In other words, in a parking lot outside our favorite restaurant, Caitlin was Jesus to me. She gave voice to her truest self while being aware of my truest self, knowing it might create conflict, and assuring me it could still lead to real wholeness in the end. She was a true peacemaker, instead of a peacefaker.

Of course, this kind of peacemaking is way harder work than peacefaking. We might have to push back against our belief that peace is the absence of conflict. We might have to push back against companions who have a vested interest in our peacefaking, because it's how they keep us quiet. We might have to face all our own fears about conflict and rejection. We might have to get better at holding our ground while honoring the ground everyone else is standing on as well. We *will* have to get better at tuning in to our true self, and increasingly wise about distinguishing it from our protective false self. Much of the struggle of exiting our chrysalis revolves around this process of discernment. Clarity here does not come easy. It comes through years of mess and mistakes and growth and grace.

As Kelly and I crest the hill and I catch my breath, I'm thinking about Caitlin's bravery the night before, and I decide to tell Kelly I can't go at our normal pace for the remainder of the ride. I tell her doing so would leave me lifeless for the rest of the holiday. I apologize for holding her back and brace myself for her disappointment. She just smiles back at me, and in her smile, our companionship is made whole. She tells me she's happy to let me take the lead and to go at whatever pace works for me.

Sometimes, it turns out, love goes the *slow* way.

When you let your true self speak up in the midst of your companionship—even at the risk of creating conflict, *especially* at the risk of creating conflict—you are giving your companionship a chance to become true, a chance to become whole, a chance to become *shalom*. Of course, it is just a chance. Kelly has not always responded so agreeably to my true self. Nor I to hers. There are no guarantees. However, there is also no other way. May you speak up. And may you give you and your companions a chance to ride together, truly, through all of it. The mess and the mistakes. The growth and the grace.

12

CERTAINTY

Sell your cleverness and
buy bewilderment.

RUMI

WE ARE RUNNING LATE FOR SCHOOL because one kid spilled cereal on himself at the last minute, one kid had not quite exactly told the whole-truth-and-nothing-but-the-truth about having brushed his teeth—in other words, he hadn't brushed his teeth at all, perhaps for days—and the last one had wanted to wear pink and purple to school, but all her purple shirts were already in the hamper, and this had resulted in a long and complex negotiation in which I had argued that the small purple hearts on her socks were enough purple for one day. We finally pile into the minivan, I turn the key, and the engine doesn't turn over. With dread, I check the headlights and, sure enough, they had been left on overnight. The minivan is Kelly's car, and she can be a little absentminded about some of the smaller details in life—like headlights. So, I return to the house, where I tell her I need her help to jump-start the van, while subtly suggesting all the ways she has just ruined my day, and probably my life. At first, she's apologetic. Then she says ten words upon which the morning, and our companionship, will hinge: "Wait. I didn't drive the car last night. *You* did."

Huh.

That is the word-sound that happens in my head when I bump up against this protection called certainty. Of course, certainty isn't a bad thing. In fact, we're designed to be certain. When we encounter a dangerous situation, we are meant to make quick decisions without question, using simplified representations of the world called schemas. These mental shortcuts keep us safe. "Huh" is what happens when this safety mechanism backfires. "Huh" is what happens when certainty and fallibility meet. "Huh" is also a moment of choice. Do I double down on my certainty that Kelly is the problem here by saying something like, "Yeah, well, you're *usually* the one who leaves the headlights on," or do I take this opportunity to push back against this protection?

The choosing and the pushing are usually a struggle.

I have opportunities for this kind of struggle all the time. For example, when I send a "perfect" first draft to my wife or to my editor and they suggest it is, um, slightly less than perfect. Huh. Or when a client tells me that my brilliant intervention from the previous week was actually a little hurtful. Huh. Or when I take away Aidan's phone as a consequence for missing homework assignments, and he points out relatively calmly that I'm looking at last quarter's grades. Huh.

Moments of uncertainty accumulate, if you let them. As they gather, they invite you out from behind your expectations into the open air where true companionship is possible. Some moments are smaller than others, of course—they come and go and are forgotten by the end of the day. Then there are those big, blessed moments of uncertainty, the kind that rock you to your core, reminding you that you don't know everything, or perhaps anything, for sure.

I had one of those big moments several summers ago.

My expectations had formed three decades earlier. Around that time, I was a kindergartner, rehearsing Bible trivia every Sunday morning in the basement of a small church. Every time we got a question right we got a point. One Sunday, I'd accrued enough points to pick a prize, and I chose a rock painted in the colors of the rainbow. It was a mixed metaphor. The colors were meant to depict God's promise to Noah after the devastating flood God had rained upon the earth. The rock itself was meant to depict faith. Jesus had said somewhere that our belief in him must be as solid as a rock, lest we build our life on shifting sand and get ourselves washed away by deadly storms. For a six-year-old, all the scary storms in the Bible were a little disconcerting. However, there was something even more troubling. The rock was a mixed metaphor for that *entire church*.

On the surface of it, the church was all rainbow colors— smiles and singing and prizes. Yet everything beneath the surface was hard and cold, like a stone. Every week, after Sunday school, I'd join my parents for adult church. I remember the pastor stalking the stage while waving his Bible in the air, shouting about a dark cloud hanging over our town. More storms, more fear. Hellfire and brimstone. Believe the right thing, without a doubt, lest your eternity be *thrown* into doubt.

That sort of stuff lingers inside of you, no matter how much time has passed.

Three decades later, I was thumbing through the Bible and I came across the passage in which Jesus teaches about where to build your house. It goes like this: "Therefore everyone who hears these words of mine and puts them into practice is like a wise man who built his house on the rock." It was different than I remembered. For decades, I'd thought Jesus had said you needed to *believe* in him in order to avoid the storms, but he'd said no such thing. He'd simply recommended *living* like him. It wasn't about making a statement of faith; it was about taking *steps* of faith. I'd been trying to get somewhere in this vehicle called faith for many years now, and it was clear my childhood church had left me with a dead battery from the very beginning. The protective part of me wanted to walk right into that place and lament about how it had ruined my faith, and probably my life.

So, I entered the name of that old church into Google Maps.

I got in the car and, thirty minutes later, as I got close to the church, I began to remember things. For instance, I remembered the dilapidated factories we'd pass every week. They're still there. They're still dilapidated. I remembered passing those factories one Sunday with Steely Dan's "Reeling in the Years" playing on the radio. Three decades later, I turned onto the narrow country road on which the church stands, and it came into view. It was smaller than I remembered. It was a little worse for wear, too, like most of rural America these days.

I don't think there is a formula for making big moments of uncertainty like that happen to you. They take you off-guard, and they are all the more transformative for the lack of warning. However, I do believe you can cultivate smaller moments of uncertainty, and those smaller moments can add up to some big transformation in you and in your companionship. All you have to do is let your companions do one small thing. You have to let them *surprise* you. To paraphrase the poet Rumi, you have to trade your clever certainty for some blessed bewilderment.

Put simply, you have to practice curiosity instead of certainty. You've been looking at your loved ones through the dirty window of your expectations. Raise the window. Put aside your expectations. See clearly. Watch attentively. Become aware of what is *actually* happening between you, rather than what you *assume* will happen. Don't draw conclusions. Be observant. Be patient. Be persistent. Don't look away. Eventually and inevitably, your companions will do something to make you go "huh."

For instance, Kelly and I go through rough seasons. Things get cooler in our companionship. Words take on a bite. The space between us expands. For years, I thought I knew exactly what I could expect from her during such seasons. I expected her to hold a grudge, to get icier. Now, I try to let her surprise me and, sure enough, she always does. I notice laughter I ignored before. I notice a gentle touch I failed to feel before. Sometimes, I simply notice the absence of the worst thing I expected and, in that space, I see something else. I see her effort to reconnect with me.

In the English language, we often say "uh-huh" when we mean yes. We say "uh-uh" when we mean no. "Huh" is neither. It is not agreement. It is not disagreement. It is simply an opportunity to *not know*. To be bewildered. To be uncertain. To question our own perspective and even our own perceptions. "Huh" is the first sound in the word *humble*. Perhaps that is no coincidence. True companionship asks us to trade the safety of our certainty for the risk and reward of humility. "Huh" is also the first sound in the word *hug*. Perhaps that is no coincidence either.

Perhaps "huh" is the sound that makes every true embrace possible.

13

YESSING

*When you say "yes" to others, make sure
you are not saying "no" to yourself.*

PAULO COELHO

I THINK I WAS A GOOD DAD when we had one kid, a mediocre dad to two kids, and now with three kids my parenting sometimes borders on unhinged. If we saved a nickel for their future therapy every time I got overwhelmed by their requests, we wouldn't need a therapy jar—we'd need a therapy garbage can. The industrial-sized kind, with wheels.

Lunchtime in the summertime has almost cost me my sanity on a number of occasions. One wants a peanut butter and jelly sandwich, another wants a cheese sandwich, and a third wants turkey. No, I say, we're all having cheese sandwiches. One wants provolone, one cheddar, one muenster. "Cheddar for everybody," I cry, with madness in my eyes. They see it, and silence follows. For approximately one minute.

Then, the oldest asks for permission to do something with his friends that he has never been allowed to do and never *will* be allowed to do and he wants to debate it to death, while the middle one is jonesing for his daily hour of video-game time and is asking me every two-and-a-half seconds to log him on to the family computer, while the little one is begging me to get a box of dolls down from the top shelf of her closet so she can make her bedroom look like a toy-store tragedy. I try to do it all at once and, as I'm lifting the box from the shelf, an odor wafts through the bedroom door.

Burning cheese sandwiches.

It would be easy to blame this on my kids, but the truth is, it's not about them. It's about me. As many spiritual teachers have said, the way you do one thing is the way you do all things, and I have a habit of trying to help everyone with everything. For years, I did this with Kelly too. If she had a request, my answer was yes. It was my default mode, because it was one of my default protections. Indeed, it is one of the most common relationship protections. I call it *yessing*.

Yessing is the tendency to say yes to every request without first filtering it through our truest and wisest self. On the surface of it, this might look a lot like peacefaking, but there is a key difference: whereas peacefaking is usually intended to avoid disagreement, yessing is intended to avoid abandonment. In other words, I'm a decent care-*giver*, but I'm not very comfortable with being a care-*receiver* because deep down I believe people will only keep me around if I keep on giving to them. I figure if people can depend on me for help without having to burn too many calories in return, they'll do the mental math and decide to stick with me.

I remember a time when a friend took our daughters to dance class and I offered to pick up his daughter in return. He declined with a mischievous smile, saying, "I want you in my debt." He didn't really. He was just calling me out on one of my protections. He was telling me he was going to stick with me, no matter how little I help him. Years later, he is one of my most closest companions.

When yessing is our protection, we try to keep the scales of social indebtedness tipped well away from us. Deep down, we're unsure if people really *like* us, so we hope to keep them around by making sure they really *owe* us. We compensate for doubts about our worthiness by making sure there is no doubt about our *easiness*. Yessers try not to have any needs and are *sure* not to have any *wants*. However, as most yessers will tell you, this is ultimately unsustainable. When you give everything and require nothing in return, you invite relationships in which your energy is drained but never restored. Inevitably, you burn out. Before you do, though, you might *lash* out, as the resentment about your imbalanced life accidentally boils over. Many yessers manage to keep a lid on this resentment by drinking, which is one reason so many people watch the clock, counting down the minutes until 5:00 p.m.

They've been yessing all day.

Growing resentment toward the demands of your companions may be a sign they are demanding too much, but it's just as likely a sign that somewhere along the way you abdicated your healthy boundaries, including your responsibility to care for yourself first, your right to ask for reciprocity, and your reasons for having a separate self. You *can* go back to that fork in the road and reclaim the practice of healthy boundaries, but it will require risk. It could lead to rejection. It might leave you particularly lonely again for a while. However, in the long run it will be worth it, because along the path of healthy boundaries you will discover one of the great eventual gifts of true companionship: *mutuality*.

At the very least, you won't burn the cheese sandwiches quite as often.

For a while, I resented my kids' many demands. Then I finally realized it wasn't their fault. A generation doesn't become selfish on its own. It becomes selfish when the generation raising it becomes *self-less*, which is to say without a separate self of its own. With all of my yessing, I was accidentally *training* them to be entitled. I knew if I was going to restore my sanity, I would need to restore the balance in my relationship to these little companions of mine. Sure, I'd risk them being upset with me. They might accuse me of not loving them. They might become adolescents who rebel with lots of drugs and sex and then move to a coast and never speak to me again, nor let me meet my grandchildren.

So be it.

I implemented two new ideas into our summertime routine, and it saved my sanity. The first was a suggestion box. Not a literal one, of course. A metaphorical one. Now, when my kids ask something of me, I don't consider it an obligation. I consider it an *option*. As the requests roll in, I explain to them I can only take one at a time, and I can only respond to their requests for, say, the next sixty minutes. Then the suggestion box will be closed for an hour while dad checks in with his own soul's suggestions. The suggestion box is teaching my kids to stop seeing me as a lever they pull for a reward they want, and to start seeing me as a human who loves them but also loves himself. Equally.

In addition to a suggestion box, I started holding powwows. I use that Native American term with great respect. It is derived from the Narragansett word *powwaw*, meaning "spiritual leader." It is a practice of gathering for meetings, dancing, socializing, and celebrating. So, my kids and I come together at the beginning of a summer day, and we have a powwow. We play music, and each of us shares all the things we want to do that day. Anything goes. A trip to Europe? Sure, put it on the list. Then, I take responsibility for scheduling out the day with the goal of honoring at least one request from each of us, including my own. So far, Europe has never made the final cut.

I do this with my kids in the summertime, and I'm trying to do this with all of my people all of the time—my friends, the boards I serve on, the clients I counsel, the employees I manage, the readers I correspond with, the event organizers I work with. Rather than frantically trying to grant every request, I hold a powwow in my heart, and into each day I schedule a relatively equal balance of give and take. Some days, I might even ask more of my people than they ask of me. In other words, I practice no-ing, and I let myself be *difficult*.

For years, Kelly had no idea how much I was needing from her. Then, finally, I stopped yessing her, and I started setting boundaries with her. At first, I was overly aggressive about it. Learning to set boundaries is like learning to drive a car. It's herky-jerky at first—too much gas, then too much brakes, and so on, until eventually you get used to the pedals. Slowly, I learned how to express my needs without attacking her. As I did so, she learned about all the ways I need help too. Now, sometimes she can tell when I'm holding back even better than I can, not because she can read my mind, but because I've pushed my heart beyond its protections, where she can see it. For instance, from time to time I'll let my boundaries go again. I'll get over-booked and overwhelmed and begin to feel like all the respon-sibility for everything lies with me. I start to get quiet and re-sentful. In this lull before the storm, I will regularly get a text from Kelly saying something like, "I want you to know you are not alone. We are here to help you. Let us know if there is any-thing we can do."

And just like that, in a little blue bubble on my phone, *philia*.

14

COMPETITION

*A flower does not think of competing with
the flower next to it. It just blooms.*

ZEN SHIN

ANOTHER SUMMER, ANOTHER WEEK at the beach. It's
one of our most treasured family traditions, and within the
big tradition are many smaller ones: morning bike rides, afternoon
jigsaw puzzles, evening dance parties, and perhaps most cherished
of all, lunch on the beach. Around noontime, while the kids play
in the waves, I head to the boardwalk for a bucket of french fries
the size of a small trash can, sizzling hot, drenched in vinegar,
sprinkled with salt. When I return, the kids are asked to approach
the beach blanket carefully, so as not to kick sand into the fries.
Two of our children almost always comply. The middle one,
though, is a little too much like me. He's competitive.

For Quinn, this isn't a leisurely lunchtime moment. This is a
moment in which he might be left with fewer french fries than
his brother or sister. To him, it's a competition for resources, so
he likes to take the quickest route to them. One day, he runs

right across the blanket, accidentally kicking sand into the bucket of fries. When it comes to food, a little sand goes a long way. In his race to win more french fries, he has ruined them.

Competition works the same way in companionship, ruining it, making it inedible, unlivable. Competition and connection—like anger and fear—are mutually exclusive intentions. You can't be competitive and connective in the same moment. This truth isn't always obvious. For instance, when Quinn's soccer team is playing a game, they will quickly take a knee when a player on the other team gets injured, a generous show of compassion. However, in the moment they take the knee, they *quit competing*. When play resumes, if they remain compassionate, they will be uncompetitive. Similarly, men often believe they are connecting in the midst of competition—athletics and card games come to mind—but the truth is they don't connect *during* the competition; they connect *about* the competition. They compete, then laugh about it, then go back to competing. This is why women are more likely to choose book clubs over poker nights. They're choosing connection over competition.

Some of the highest achieving people I know are disturbed by this idea. They want *deeply* to be more connected to their companions and their colleagues, but they worry that doing so will rob them of their competitive edge. They fear connection will cost them production. I'm always happy to reassure them that, as competition gives way to connection in their life, they will not achieve less; in fact, they will probably achieve more. When we trade dominance for *excellence*, we also receive balance and peacefulness and sustainability. We can usually produce more in the midst of harmony than chaos and achieve more with the glad support of our companions than with their re-sentful resistance. Unlike dominance, excellence has space for connection and compassion within it.

Having said that, competition is a particularly effective pro-tection, so it can be particularly difficult to leave behind. Com-panions frequently compete about who was right, what really happened, how it was really said, why someone did what they did, who is contributing the most value, and who is creating the most problems. Couples usually call a couples therapist with their true selves, hoping to take a knee and reclaim their sense of compassion and connection.

Nevertheless, almost every partner shows up for therapy with their protective self prepared for competition: they each want the therapist to declare them the winner in their ongoing con-tests. While fighting for victory, they miss out on the beauty their hearts most desire.

Less than eighteen hours after Quinn accidentally spoiled the french fries, the kids and I are back at the beach for another annual tradition: watching the sun rise. As always, the star rises slowly, in a long labor of light. Like the first small contractions in the birthing of a new day, the dark sky above the ocean gradually begins to brighten from black into blue, and the sea gradually begins its morning-long transition from navy into turquoise. Then, eventually, like the sharper contractions of labor, the morning sky gets etched in hotter colors—reds and oranges and burning purples.

Meanwhile, Quinn is witnessing none of it. He is busy building a sand castle in the cool morning sand. I ask him to look up, but he is once again in a hurry. In this moment, I don't think Quinn is competing with anyone. He isn't trying to build a better castle than the kid two umbrellas down, because at this time of day, we're alone on the beach. No, I think Quinn is simply exhibiting one inevitable consequence of competition: a mind stuck in *doing* mode. For the competitive mind, busyness becomes a way of life because it's the way to beat everyone else. The competitive mind gathers momentum as its addiction to doing grows.

Sadness wells up within me, not for him, but for me. He's young. He'll have plenty of sunrises to witness, but I've probably got less than half of mine remaining. How much of my life and my people am I going to miss checking items off of my competitive to-do list? While I wonder this, the star continues to rise slowly—until it doesn't. Suddenly, like the blazing crown of a celestial baby's head, its curve appears on the horizon. Caitlin squeals with delight, as the birthing of a new day accelerates. Like the final push of childbirth, the sun appears to climb the horizon in an instant. We stand at the edge of the land, and as Quinn builds his castle, the rest of us are silenced by wonder.

Eventually, Aidan breaks the reverent hush with a bit of wisdom that makes my eyes as wet and salty as the ocean itself. "This is the point of life, Dad. To marvel at the beauty of it." He sounds like the great Christian theologian C. S. Lewis, who wrote, "We do not want merely to see beauty, though, God knows, even that is bounty enough. We want something else which can hardly be put into words—to be united with the beauty we see, to pass into it, to receive it into ourselves, to bathe in it, to become a part of it."

This moment lingers with me, and for the rest of the beach vacation, I watch people—including myself—rushing to-and-fro in every direction, competing for the best deals on beach sandals and a spot at the front of the carnival-ride line. Their energy is frenetic. In contrast, I also observe people who are truly on vacation. They have vacated this chrysalis of competition. They murmur to each other on benches. They stand hand in hand as evening fades to night. They hold doors for strangers and smile at each other in passing. As I pay attention, I become aware of a light at the center of my own competitive and hurried darkness. It is a light called *presence*. It is a star rising slowly within me.

It has been several years since we watched that long, slow sunrise. For a while, I worked hard to push my way out of all my competitive doing. It was, ironically, pretty slow going, because when you work hard at not working so hard, you've simply found a new thing to work on. When you try to stop all your doing by doing something new, you've simply found a different reason to do something. In other words, there is nothing you can *do* to leave your competitiveness behind. Rather, you have to allow the *opposite* of doing. You have to learn how to *not do anything*.

The true opposite of winning is not losing, it's simply *being*.

The idea of a national yoga championship is laughable, because exercises that focus on the cultivation of nondoing are inherently noncompetitive, and there are a million little ways to practice the art of simply being. Most of them are related to the practice of presence and the discipline of mindfulness. A great little app called Headspace has helped me along the way. I now try to spend as much time focused on my breathing as on my winning. I've also been helped by many contemplative mentors, including Thomas Merton, Henri Nouwen, and Richard Rohr. I recommend you find your own guide into being.

Kelly has helped me most of all, though. More specifically, my hope for connection with her has replaced most of my hopeless competition with her. So, when I'm around her, I try to quit obsessing about my to-*do* list and settle into my to-*be* list instead. Sometimes I'm more successful than others. For instance, recently I was beginning a hectic week by hustling out of the house, thinking about how busy my week was going to be (Read: how much *busier* than hers. #competition). She stopped me on the way out the door, gave me a hug, and wished me a good day. I grumbled something about the harried state of my life and then walked toward the door. As I reached for the knob, a connective voice entered my competitive mind: "She has a big day as well; why don't you wish her well too?" My hand was resting on the knob when she spoke up from behind me.

"You know," she said, "you could have wished me a good day too."

My competitive mind rose up in my defense, and I felt the urge to recite a laundry list of reasons my day would be harder than hers. Then, again, my connective heart spoke louder than my competitive mind: "She's right. She deserves your recognition too. Trade your competition for connection." I turned around, went to her, thanked her for calling me out, and wished her success in her busy day as well. She looked at me with a compassionate and playful smile and said, "Aw, you're forty-three years old and you're starting to get it." Once again, she was right. Love goes the long way and the slow way to get to the french fries. *Philia* doesn't compete with the flower next to it.

It simply blooms.

15

WITHDRAWAL

*Human beings are born solitary, but everywhere
they are in chains—daisy chains—of interactivity.
Social actions are makeshift forms, often
courageous, sometimes ridiculous, always
strange. And in a way, every social action
is a negotiation, a compromise between
"his," "her," or "their" wish and yours.*

ANDY WARHOL

H ER EYEBROWS SHOT SO HIGH I thought they might hit
the ceiling.

Sometimes when I travel for speaking events I go alone, and
sometimes Kelly comes with me. This time, I was leading a marriage retreat for a group of couples, and Kelly was sitting in the
front row. I was in the midst of explaining this protection called
withdrawal, when her eyebrows went skyward. Usually when
she does that during an event I'm leading, it means I've omitted
an important point or miscommunicated a crucial detail. So, I
stopped midsentence and asked if she had anything to add.

Her lips grew tight and colorless as she shook her head no. "Oh come on," I insisted, "tell us what's on your mind." I thought I could see a bit of glee enter her eyes. Suddenly, I was a little unnerved. I prompted her again anyway. "Okay," she said reluctantly, "do you remember the boundary you drew with me during the break?" Now I knew where she was going with this. I was being called out for the very protection about which I was teaching: withdrawal.

Between sessions, we'd had an opportunity to go for a long and enjoyable walk, and near the end of it Kelly had raised a topic that had been bothering her. For the first time in twenty years, instead of going on our annual summer beach vacation, we were planning a trip to Portugal, because Kelly and the kids wanted to explore the homeland of their ancestors. Outwardly, I'd agreed to the trip, but inwardly I was conflicted. The well-worn routines of our typical beach vacation help me relax. When problems arise, as they always do, I usually know how to solve them, because I've usually solved them before. Not to mention, the problems happen in English. To me, Portugal sounded like a bunch of problems to solve in a language I can't comprehend.

Here's the thing, though: I wasn't peacefaking or yessing. I wasn't avoiding disagreement or abandonment. I wasn't silencing my most authentic voice. I really did want to give my family the vacation they all wanted. However, I was also unsure of my ability to do so, while pining for one of my favorite annual traditions. So, though my truest self was all-in on our trip to Portugal, another part of me was throwing a bit of a snit. Every time Kelly had asked me to sit down to plan the trip, I'd found some reason or another to cut the discussion short. On our walk, she'd confronted me about my avoidance. My response, I'm sure, would have sounded quite reasonable and rational to the outside observer. I told her she is the one proficient at Portuguese and I'm not, so my problem-solving and planning skills would be unfortunately neutralized for this trip. It was up to her. I'd gladly go on the trip, but when it came to the planning, I was totally out. Essentially, I'd told her that on this vacation there would be one parent and four kids. Basically, I withdrew from our companionship.

One of the best ways to protect against the natural but challenging give-and-take of a relationship is to pretend you aren't in one.

Of course, we all need to withdraw from time to time. For example, it is healthy to press pause on our conflict when it is destructive and unproductive. We need space to gather ourselves. This doesn't sever the companionship; it *preserves* it. And of course it's okay to keep parts of ourselves *to* ourselves. Having a companion doesn't mean you can't have privacy. It simply means your privacy is intentional and wise—it is always in the service of deepening connection rather than deception. Kelly was calling me out on a kind of withdrawal that was decreasing our connection. It's called separation. Secrets and silence are two others . . .

Several years ago, the kids got home from school on a hot autumn afternoon and asked if I would take them for ice cream. I knew Kelly had done so the day before, and I knew they didn't need ice cream two days in a row, but I also knew I was tired of Kelly being the cool parent while I was the *rule* parent. So, I took them for ice cream. Then, when we got home, I took all of the empty containers and buried them as far as I could in the kitchen trash, way beneath the day's breakfast and lunch debris. I actually did that. I planned to keep their second consecutive day of afternoon ice cream a secret.

This is a subtle form of relationship withdrawal. We slightly sever the relationship with little secrets, like what we just ordered from Amazon. We make bigger breaks by burying bigger things, like our dreams and desires and dysfunctions. We hide parts of ourselves we believe are too weird to be understood and parts we believe are too flawed to be accepted. Knowing ourselves to be one of a kind—in ways both good and embarrassing —we decide it's wise to remain inside our chrysalis, perhaps even romanticizing it as individualism, autonomy, and freedom. When this protection is habitual, we may have people, but our people never really have *us*. We live elusively amongst our loved ones. Our companions wonder why we are so hard to know. We aren't inclined to tell them. But tell them we must, if we hope to trade our protective withdrawal for some connective confession. We don't have to immediately tell everything, but we do have to start telling something. Our secrets keep a ceiling on our capacity for closeness.

May we raise the roof.

Secrets are a common form of withdrawal, but silence is even more ubiquitous. It is usually exhibited by exactly one partner in a pair. It often happens in the midst of conflict, when one member of the relationship goes quiet and refuses to engage.

Like my conversation with Kelly, it is not meant to avoid disagreement. In fact, it sends a very clear signal of very real disagreement. It is also not meant to avoid abandonment. Indeed, it *promotes* a sense of abandonment in the other, which triggers them to demand more connection, which simply produces more withdrawal, and so on. Relationship experts call this either the "demand-withdraw" or the "pursuer-distancer" communication pattern. Whatever you call it, almost every couple who presents for couples' therapy exhibits it, and they are well aware of it. However, what the withdrawer is usually not aware of is this: the most powerful person in a relationship is the one most willing to leave it.

This is a surprise, because usually the withdrawer doesn't *feel* powerful; they feel *overwhelmed*. They may feel like their companion is always trying to control them with words or dominate them with conversation. They say things like, "I'm just trying to get a little space, for crying out loud." To achieve this, they withdraw from the dialogue. They clam up. They may still be present physically, but they have left the relationship emotionally, and there is nothing their partner can do to draw them out. That is power.

Ironically, where the demand-withdraw communication pattern is prevalent, both companions usually report exactly the same feeling: the conversation was making them anxious. However, the pattern developed because they have diametrically opposed ways of trying to soothe that fear. Demanders seek conversation and connection to soothe their anxiety, while withdrawers seek silence and solitude to calm themselves down. To change this divisive pattern, demanders have to ease up a little, and withdrawers have to check back in a little. For a withdrawer, silence is safe. Staying engaged is both the risk *and* the reward of true companionship.

Good boundaries are, of course, a very good thing. For instance, when our protection is yessing, building healthier boundaries is actually an *essential* thing. However, when one of your go-to protections is withdrawal, there's a good chance your boundaries have gotten *too* good. In other words, your boundaries leave little space for your companions to have boundaries of their own. When their boundaries ask something of you, you think they're unreasonable. Requests for the intertwining of your lives are viewed as interference with *your* life. Requests for compromise are viewed as criticism. Requests for growth are viewed as condemnation. From within your protective withdrawal, you may even see their healthiest boundaries as demands to be different, rather than requests for relationship. You cling to your own routines and habits and patterns.

You cling to the beach rather than planning for Portugal.

In the end, this kind of separation is mostly just protection against the challenges of threading two distinct and delightful souls together. Pushing our way out of it is hard work, but it can also be beautiful work. The art of compromise is the distinction between who we are and what we do: our truest companions are not asking us to compromise who we *are*; they're asking us to compromise what we *do* with who we are. This isn't interference or criticism or condemnation. This is a reasonable negotiation of boundaries. In the words of Andy Warhol, this is the often courageous, sometimes ridiculous, always strange negotiation of wishes. This is the necessary dance of companionship.

I told Kelly I'd gladly help her plan Portugal,

her eyebrows relaxed,

and everyone watched,

as we danced.

16

FIXING

*When care is our first concern, cure can
be received as a gift. Often we are not
able to cure, but we are always able
to care. To care is to be human.*

HENRI NOUWEN

Aidan procrastinated. Again.

Summer is just around the corner, and the end of Aidan's first year of high school is quickly approaching. He's mostly focused on the end and mostly not focused on what comes right before the end: final exams. So, the night before his two hardest finals, he's scrambling to cram geometric theorems and Spanish conjugations into his already full mind, and he's close to losing it. I try to be patient with him, but to be honest, my patience for his procrastination ran out somewhere in the middle of middle school.

A day later, with the two exams behind him, and that horrible post-exam, I-think-I-flunked-it feeling in his stomach, he comes to me and asks me how to fix this pattern of procrastination in his life. He wants a list of things he can do to prevent this scenario from playing out again next year, and I'm a shrink, so I've got all sorts of tools in my toolbox that I could take out and hand to him. I'd love to do so because, as a psychologist, it's in my nature to fix things. That's why I became a therapist in the first place. However, over the years, I've learned that some things don't need to be fixed, they need to be *felt*.

Sometimes, feeling *is* fixing.

So, I remind him that all of our past attempts to fix his procrastination have been futile. I suggest there is no study plan that will prevent him from procrastinating next year. In fact, if I give him a plan right now, it will help him to move past this terrible feeling in the pit of his stomach too quickly. He will focus on fixing instead of feeling, and he will miss out on everything the feeling has to teach him. I tell him the best motivation for not procrastinating next year is to let himself thoroughly feel the results of having procrastinated this year. Unpleasant feelings are not usually our enemy. They are signposts, telling us which direction we want to go next. We have to take the time to read them carefully.

I've learned this lesson over and over again as a clinical psychologist. For instance, I used to treat depression in my clients as an intense feeling that needed to be fixed. Then, about a decade ago, I realized my own depression wasn't merely an intense feeling but rather an intense *exhaustion* resulting from suppressing all of my *other* feelings. It takes a lot of mental effort to bottle up our anger, avoid our fears, or hide our sadness and shame. In other words, sometimes the way to start fixing depression is to start *feeling* everything else.

Sometimes, feeling *is* fixing.

Similarly, as a couples therapist, I used to try fixing marriages by fixing their fighting. I'd teach communication skills, challenge cognitive errors such as mind reading, and develop rules of engagement. All of this helped a little. However, I began to notice some couples were not helped at all by these methods, and in those marriages there was a common thread: one of the partners got paid to fix things all day. They were surgeons, scientists, and CEOs. All day long, they were asked to fix things, and they were good at it, so when they came home they just kept trying to fix things. A spouse was sad? Here's how to be happy. A teenager was struggling socially? Here's how to be popular. A child was anxious? Here's how to be fearless. But it almost always broke bad for these folks. Their people needed to know it was okay to *not* be fixed.

Henri Nouwen writes,

Care is something other than cure. *Cure* means "change." A doctor, a lawyer, a minister, a social worker—they all want to use their professional skills to bring about changes in people's lives. They get paid for whatever kind of cure they can bring about. But cure, desirable as it may be, can easily become violent, manipulative, and even destructive if it does not grow out of care. Care is being with, crying out with, suffering with, feeling with. Care is compassion. It is claiming the truth that the other person is my brother or sister, human, mortal, vulnerable, like I am.

Following Nouwen's guidance, I shifted my first focus in therapy from fixing problems to feeling emotions, and I discovered that sometimes care *is* the cure. Sometimes, feeling *is* fixing.

On countless occasions, this has helped my own marriage as well. In fact, the day after Aidan agreed to feel the effects of his recent procrastination, I got a call from Kelly. My normally unshakable wife sounded quite shaken. It was three days before that first half Ironman triathlon of hers. For months, I had sensed her anxiety about the race floating around in the depths of her, and it had finally come to the surface. She'd been having pain in her shoulders from her training swims, and she was worried about her ability to stay afloat and to stay safe in the open waters of a choppy lake, with thousands of competitors swimming over each other. She was also scared about having to ride a bike farther than she'd ever ridden before, with a literal pain in her butt resulting from all of her training rides. She was calling me in the hopes of identifying a cure for her fears. She was desperately searching for a fix.

She wondered if she should try another practice swim in more open water. She wondered if she should tinker with her bike seat and try another long ride. I was tempted to offer several solutions. Instead, I wondered aloud if she could do what Jesus did when his friend Lazarus died. Though Jesus knew he would soon fix the situation by resurrecting Lazarus, he paused anyway to feel his feelings. It's the shortest verse in the Bible: "Jesus wept." I suggested she simply pause for a moment, rest for a day, give her body a break, and let herself feel her feelings. In other words, I told her to care for her heart rather than trying to cure her body. Over the next few days, she made a companion of her fear. She cared for it instead of trying to cure it.

The feeling *was* the fixing.

The desire to fix our world and our people is a beautiful thing. It can lead to incredible discoveries, invaluable solutions, and priceless cures. However, it can also become a new problem unto itself, a way of relating that leaves everyone feeling like a quandary to be solved, a diseased to be cured, or an inconvenience to be altered. Furthermore, when our attempts to fix our people become fruitless, we get tempted to shift our attention to problems that *can* actually be resolved. Lawns to mow. Rooms to paint. Diapers to change. Jobs that reward our mindset. Sometimes we'll even go searching for someone who *is* fond of our fixing, a mister or mistress perhaps.

What if, instead, we put feeling before fixing?

Our lives are a little like Kelly's half Ironman—a race we're not totally prepared for and might never finish the way we hope. Sure, it's safer to stay in your head, coaching your loved ones to the finish line from the sideline. However, it's lovelier to settle into your heart so you can get into the race with them, feeling all the same fear and exhaustion and exhilaration they are feeling. When you run alongside someone, you don't tell them how to quit feeling the ache; you feel the ache *with* them. You don't encourage them to feel better while they're running; you simply encourage them to keep going.

And your presence alongside them becomes the greatest encouragement of all.

17

HELICOPTERING

Be crumbled.
So wild flowers will come up where you are.
You have been stony for too many years.
Try something different.
Surrender.

RUMI

THIS SPRING, IT HAS RAINED almost every Tuesday morning. Typically, in the springtime, after a long Chicago winter, I enjoy resuming my Tuesday morning walks to Starbucks for a cup of coffee. Several weeks into this waterlogged season, however, I complained to my favorite barista that, thanks to yet another rainy morning, I'd had to drive for coffee *again*. She was having none of it. "You don't need a change of weather," she said, "you need a change of attitude. The rain is an invitation to splash in the puddles." She smiled and walked away. In that moment, she was more than a barista. She was a guru.

This spring I've been avoiding the puddles on the sidewalk, but the truth is I've spent most of my forty-some years trying to sidestep the puddles in my *life*—ordinary human puddles like disappointment and pain. However, I don't just try to *avoid* the puddles in my life, I also try to *prevent* them. In this, I am not alone. A new phrase has emerged in pop culture over the last decade: helicopter parent. It has even made the leap from pop culture into the *Oxford English Dictionary*, in which it is defined as "a parent who takes an overprotective or excessive interest in the life of their child or children."

Helicoptering is different than fixing. Fixing is about solving problems *after* the fact, whereas helicoptering is about preventing them altogether. When helicoptering is our go-to protection, we are living according to the old adage, "An ounce of prevention is worth a pound of cure." Of course, the instinct for prevention has led to important progress—seat belts and bike helmets and bug spray come to mind. Trying to prevent the puddles in our humanity has resulted in a bunch of good things like vaccines and vitamin supplements and the wisdom to bite my tongue when I'm about to act like a jerk. However, it is just as likely to produce a bunch of worry, and it isn't a huge leap from worrying to helicoptering. Worry is what happens when you *want* to prevent the puddles in your life, whereas helicoptering is what happens when you *try* to prevent the puddles in your life.

Helicoptering is worry with propellers on.

Helicoptering can protect us for a while, but it almost always crashes and burns, because when you're always trying to prevent *every* puddle—or trying to prevent puddles that are unpreventable—it can accidentally cause more problems than it could ever prevent. For example, helicopter parents are less likely to let their young kids play outdoors in order to prevent injury or kidnapping, and more likely to complete their teenager's college applications in order to prevent rejection or failure. However, where this kind of preventive parenting is prevalent, we find kids who lack resilience and adult children who fail to launch. The 2019 college admissions scandal—in which a number of affluent and famous parents rigged their kids' admissions to prestigious schools—is the natural conclusion to a lifetime of helicopter parenting.

Parents aren't the only ones who engage in this protection, though. In fact, it's only in the last several decades that parenting has been imbued with this imperative to prevent every puddle in the lives of our children. By contrast, helicopter *companioning* has been around much longer. We companions have been helicoptering our partners and spouses and siblings and friends for millennia. I'll speak for myself here, and I'll speak about my marriage specifically. With Kelly, it seems there are three puddles I'm always trying tirelessly to prevent: death, divorce, and disappointment.

At night, Kelly is as blind as a bat. I was once in the car with her after dark when she drove up a highway on-ramp, thinking it was an off-ramp. So, when she is driving home alone at night, especially over a long distance, I helicopter the heck out of her. I ask her to call me when she departs for home, and then I refresh her location on Find My iPhone way too many times, just to make sure the car is still moving. When she tells me about a suspicious-looking new spot on her skin and then procrastinates about calling the dermatologist, it drives me crazy. I've never made the appointment for her; I've just helicoptered her into it.

By the time she gets to the doctor, I'm guessing married life versus the afterlife is feeling like a bit of a toss-up for her. We helicopter our loved ones' safety in a thousand little ways. The Life360 app is a great example. It would probably be best if we did a 180 on these helicoptering habits.

Then there's divorce. If I'm completely honest, there's a small part of me that still wonders why Kelly chose me and continues to choose me every day. That part of me helicopters her, not for fear of losing her to *death*, but for fear of losing her to someone *else*. Every once in a while, when I can't reach her, I'll check her location on my phone and find she isn't where I thought she'd be. The urge to helicopter kicks in. The problem is, I'd be using my propellers to hold on to her, but those kinds of propellers only propel our companions away from us. Generally, friends and family don't love to be hovered and smothered. In our fear of losing our people, we can increase the odds of doing so.

In my efforts to prevent the puddle called disappointment, I've ruined my fair share of special occasions by helicoptering them. Anniversary dinners. Mother's Day mornings. The last day of almost every vacation. The ordinary moments in which I hope for quick connection but mess it up with my protection. With only one shot at it, I want it all to go perfectly. I want her to be happy. I want to make a memory. Unfortunately, perfectionism has way too much turbulence in it for smooth helicoptering. There are too many messy moments in the space of an hour—let alone an evening or a day—for it all to go perfectly. In recent years, Kelly and I have adopted a mantra: everything breaks.

It's a balm for my helicoptering mind.

Speaking of things breaking, how about Jesus? He spent most of his adult years relatively puddle-free. He didn't need to helicopter, because he controlled the rain itself. Literally. He quieted storms while at sea. He moved atoms in the midst of miracles, dismissed diseases during healings, sent spirits away during exorcisms, and rearranged the life force itself during resurrections. Then, suddenly, in his final week, his life presents him with a puddle the size of a lake. He's just had his last supper with his closest companions. The authorities are coming to arrest him and sentence him to death, and he tells his friends his "soul is overwhelmed with sorrow to the point of death." He retreats to a garden called Gethsemane to pray.

There, he asks his heavenly Father to helicopter him.

The book of Luke says he was in such agony of spirit that "his sweat fell to the ground like great drops of blood." The longing to prevent this puddle in his life is so intense he's sweating a puddle of his own. He beseeches his heavenly Parent to intervene: "Father, if you are willing, please take this cup of suffering away from me. Yet I want your will to be done, not mine." Then, the Roman authorities come for him and his puddle deepens. He's arrested. Beaten. Tortured. Humiliated. Hung on a cross. And on the cross, he wonders aloud why his Father isn't doing a little more helicoptering, as he cries out, "My God, my God, why have you forsaken me?"

Three days later, the empty tomb shows us why. Three days later, we find out a lack of helicoptering is not a lack of companionship. Indeed, the withholding of helicoptering may be the pinnacle of *philia*. God declined to helicopter Jesus—not because death, separation, and suffering aren't *hard*, but because they aren't the *end*. Jesus' cosmic Parent knew that light comes after darkness, rising comes after falling, resilience comes after suffering, and resurrection comes after death. In Rumi's words, when we are crumbled, wild flowers will come up where we are.

I remember the day I first pushed myself well beyond my protective helicoptering. It was my birthday. It was a Friday. I'd snuck out early in the morning to a coffee shop for some reading and writing. I returned home in time to drive the school carpool. I pulled my brand-new car into the driveway, parked it, went inside to round up the kids, piled everyone into the minivan, forgot my new car was parked at an angle just behind it, and backed the minivan right into the driver's-side door. I got out with dread to survey the damage. It was bad. Earlier in the morning, I'd been writing about how you can't prevent every mess, so you might as well quit trying. You might as well do the opposite: you might as well *embrace* the messes in life. Right then and there, looking at my demolished car door, I tried something different. I surrendered to the mess. I decided I wouldn't repair the door, so it would stand as a lasting reminder to me that everything breaks and that my efforts to prevent all the breaking are also preventing all the resurrecting.

And right then and there, standing in my driveway, wild flowers came up within me.

18

AND EXCITEMENT

*The art of being happy lies in the power of
extracting happiness from common things.*

HENRY WARD BEECHER

I HAVE NO BUSINESS WRITING THIS CHAPTER.
Sometimes my clients wonder if I will be including any part of their story in my writing. I tell them I try to tell my own stories. This policy isn't about vanity; it's about *humanity*. If someone else's experience can be found within my own experience, then it can probably also be found within our larger human experience, and it is probably a story worth telling. As a rule, if I can't find a reference point for something in my own experience, then I don't write about it. In this chapter, I'm going to break my own rule.

Although each of us is likely to have a preferred protection, our chrysalis is doubtlessly woven from the threads of several different protections. I can find within me evidence of most of the protections we've already talked about. However, there is one very important protection that is entirely foreign to me. I can't fathom it. It is anathema to who I am. Fortunately, I happen to be in very close companionship with someone who epitomizes it. In this chapter, I'm going to throw my wife under the bus. Being married to a writer can be dangerous.

Currently, Kelly has seven tattoos, and each has a very specific meaning and purpose. But the truth is, they all serve the same basic function: change. Kelly *loves* change. She seeks adventure. She thrives on excitement. She inks her body every couple of years for the sake of something *new*. Most recently, she was searching for a reason to get a new tattoo and could not come up with one, so she created one. She completed that half Ironman triathlon mostly for the right to tattoo the Ironman symbol onto her body. While she trained, she continued to work her full-time job, to serve as vice president of the local school board, to be the best mother I've ever known, and she wrote a *textbook*.

Though it can be exhausting to keep up with her, none of this comes as a surprise to me. It's not as if when I met her she was lethargically ambling through life and suddenly her pace picked up. In fact, her zest for life is a big part of why I fell in love with her. I loved that she'd launched herself from her childhood home in eighth grade by applying for a scholarship to a prestigious boarding school. I loved that she'd jumped out of an airplane and studied abroad for a semester. I loved it when, several months after we met, she convinced me to buy a plane ticket for spring break in the Virgin Islands, with no plan for lodging. I loved it even more when we found an abandoned and unlocked villa in the hills with the water still running and a breathtaking view of the bay.

With Kelly, I knew exactly what I was getting. Having said that, while I love her, I also love *my* way of doing things. I love rest and relaxation. I love weekends in pajamas, and I love that beach vacation where we stick our feet in the same place in the sand all week long. I've made myself the same smoothie every morning for the last decade. I drive the same route to my office every time. I wear the same two or three outfits to work every week. I floss my teeth in the same order every day. I believe in the power of ritual, repetition, and regularity. *Not* excitement.

Sure, to some extent, this is simply a matter of healthy complementarity. In many ways, her penchant for excitement has expanded me and enriched my life. I eat sushi now. Now, I see risk as an opportunity rather than a threat, like when we decided to quit our jobs and try a new lifestyle. Nowadays, I actually like to travel. Last year, I even got a passport. This year, we're planning to go to Europe for the first time. And I can still remember that view of the bay as the sun rose in the Virgin Islands.

But it hasn't all been fun and games. It's not that Kelly is incompatible with *me*; it's that, sometimes, excitement and adventure and change are incompatible with *true companionship*. True companionship can be a long, hard grind. This doesn't mean you're doing it incorrectly. It means you're doing it *faithfully*. In the journey that is true companionship, there are long stretches of flat, boring road running all the way to the horizon. Laundry. Carpools. Small talk. Planning. Organizing. Arguing. Groceries. Diapers. Jobs. Arguing about the same things. Foibles. Peccadillos. Pet peeves. Vacuuming. Arguing about the same things again. Repetition and ritual and regularity.

Philia has more dirty dishes in it than exotic sunsets.

For someone like me, all of that repetition feels soothing. For someone like Kelly, it can feel excruciating. When excitement is your protection, most of the ordinary requirements of being human feel like a drag, like barriers between you and happiness. Indeed, this is the very experience that excitement protects against: unhappiness. Having noticed a basic sense of unhappiness early in life, especially during times of quiet, you come to the natural conclusion: if I feel my unhappiness during times of stillness and boredom, then I will find my happiness during times of activity and excitement. Pair this early experience with a nervous system that prefers a little more stimulation than the average person, and you have my wife. And my eldest son.

Aidan wants to jump out of an airplane as soon as he is legally allowed to do so. He prefers the spotlight on opening night to anywhere else in the world. If it is forbidden and not likely to kill him, he wants to try it. Schoolwork, on the other hand? Studying for tests and taking out the garbage and remembering to turn in a permission slip? In his mind, these things are boring and senseless. Why would you waste time doing anything you have already discovered will not bring you happiness? Why would you look for euphoria in something that is guaranteed not to deliver it? The apple did not fall far from the tree.

Also, these kinds of apples are proliferating. We live in a time when change and excitement have become standard fare. We can effortlessly swipe or flick to the next new thing whenever we want. No one with a mobile device need ever endure a moment of tedium. This isn't all bad, but it isn't all good either. We are more conflicted than ever before. We long for the deep,

deep satisfaction that comes with true companionship, but we have little interest in learning to endure the long seasons of boredom and the punctuated moments of unhappiness we will encounter along the way. Yes, if we push our way out of this protection, we will get to experience the thrill of flying with another. But it won't all be flying.

More often than not, *companionship* is simply resting on a bud.

Several years ago, Kelly went out of her way to paint a picture for me, words arranged in the shape of an anchor. It read, "You be the anchor that keeps my feet on the ground, I'll be the wings that keep your heart in the clouds." This was Kelly pushing her way out of her protection. Instead of insisting on the superiority of her way of being, and the meaninglessness of mine, she was telling me—and perhaps even more importantly, telling herself—there is a place for both in our relationship. I hung it in our office where we both work and where, on Saturday mornings, Kelly sits with me in our pajamas, sipping on coffee, far longer than she would prefer. Eventually, we get up, far sooner than *I'd* prefer.

And we go searching for excitement.

A LETTER TO MY WIFE

Thank You for the Moments Between the Magic

Dear M,

Your father-in-law, as you know, is a grass man.

To him, flowers and trees and flowering trees are fine, but nothing compares to a perfectly manicured lawn. When I was a kid, it drove him crazy every spring when the magnolia tree in our front yard would make a mess all over the lawn. Its petals would bloom bright and brilliant, and for a while, all of the light entering our living room would be filtered through it. The whole room glowed. Eventually, though, on some warmer than usual day, the petals would wilt and fall to the ground. For years, he diligently raked up the petals, keeping the grass under the tree as lush as possible. One year, though, he finally got so tired of the seasonal cleanup that he cut down the tree altogether.

When I think about our marriage over the years, I think of that magnolia tree.

We've had times in our companionship during which everything glowed. We've had moments of magic and days of wonder in which our love was blooming and all of life was filtered through it. However, like that magnolia tree, those seasons have never lasted. Eventually things get a little too hot, our love wilts, and there is a mess all over the lawn of our life together. Then, we have to start cleaning it up all over again.

Is it any wonder so many couples chop down their marriages instead?

M, I used to believe the goal of companionship was never-ending bloom. I wanted the seasons of magic to go on perpetually, without interruption. However, that's not how anything really works. Everything is seasonal and cyclical. There is nothing in the whole world that exists apart from the rhythm of death and resurrection. Even monarch butterflies go through three cycles of death and rebirth every season, as they migrate thousands of miles back and forth, always wintering in warm and glowing places, no butterfly from the departing generation ever a part of the arriving generation.

Even the monarch butterfly lives in this cycle of mess and magic.

I'm beginning to accept that there will never be some final moment in which I leave my chrysalis once and for all and fly with you forever. Rather, the rhythm of companionship will mean that you and I enjoy brief periods of magic and flight, followed by another season of mess and transformation, as we struggle to extricate ourselves from our protections once again. Our seasons of magic may grow longer. From time to time, it may even seem like we've arrived at our warm and glowing destination. However, I'm no longer overly attached to those moments of flight and arrival.

In the end, M, I've fallen in love with all of it.

In the end, I can finally say, thank you for the moments of magic, but thank you, too, for the moments **between** the magic. Thank you for wading into those messy moments with me, when all of the petals of our love have wilted and fallen to the ground.

*Thank you for always working with me to clean it up one more time. It's what makes me a better human being. It's what makes us stronger companions. And, always, it prepares us to enjoy the next blooming season. Now I know we will not live **happily** ever after, but we will live **humanly** ever after. Together. And that is enough.*

Indeed, it is all I could ever hope for.

Love,

F

PART 3

GROW OLD

CHERISHING YOUR TIME

WE CAN'T REALLY VALUE our companions unless we value our time.

In study after study, researchers have observed that younger people tend to have values that emphasize achievement, accumulation, and the expansion of everything, including their social network. In contrast, older people usually share values that focus on spending time with their closest friends and family and enjoying the everyday pleasures already present in their lives. In other words, it appears that, with age and experience, our priorities shift from accomplishment to companionship.

Appearances can be deceiving.

In his bestselling book *Being Mortal*, Dr. Atul Gawande describes a series of studies by Stanford psychologist Laura Carstensen that have identified why this shift in values *really* happens. In one study during the AIDS epidemic of the 1980s, young people with HIV began to mirror the values of the elderly. Similarly, in the United States following 9/11, the differences between the goals of the young and elderly were erased in the immediate aftermath of the tragedy. Two years later, during the SARS epidemic in Asia, the age differences disappeared once again. Notably, in the last two studies, once the existential crisis passed, the gap in values returned. It turns out, the discrepancy in our priorities has almost nothing to do with *age*. It has to do with *perspective*.

Carstensen performed a laboratory study with healthy individuals ranging in age from eight to ninety-three. When asked how they would choose to spend thirty minutes of time, the typical age differences were clear. However, when the subjects were asked to imagine they were about to move far away, the young began choosing as the elderly did. Next, the subjects were encouraged to imagine a medical breakthrough had added twenty years to their life. Once again, the age differences were eliminated. However, this time the *elderly* chose like the *young*. Carstensen concluded that when "horizons are measured in decades," which feels like forever to a human being, we desire achievement and self-actualization. However, when the time ahead begins to feel finite and uncertain, our focus shifts to the immediate present, to ordinary pleasures, and to our closest people. We most value our closest companions only when, as Carstensen puts it, "life's fragility is primed."

Butterflies live like their fragility is primed, as well it should be, given they typically survive only a few weeks after struggling free of their chrysalis. They spend their quickly dwindling days fluttering through an ether they can't understand, drinking nectar from already dying buds, basking in the warmth of the sun, and enjoying their companions. That's it, from start to finish. Of course, we human beings tend to have a few more responsibilities than the average butterfly, but we also have one distinct advantage over them in this regard: if we choose, we can prime life's fragility whenever we want. We can cherish our time.

According to science, it's the only way to truly cherish our companions.

A LETTER TO MY WIFE

The Whole Thing Is Inconceivable

Dear M,

You were downstairs amongst the children's books, and I was upstairs amongst the adult books, when time collapsed in on itself.

Ours is a small-town library, more than a century old. To you, I suppose, the fragrance of the place is unremarkable, but I grew up in this space. My grandmother was a librarian here. To me, it smells like timelessness. The mere scent of it can transport me back to some of my earliest memories. This morning, though, it was the long reading tables in the main room that took me back. They're the same tables that lined the room when I was younger, solid and heavy slabs of wood, the likes of which are rarely seen anymore. As I was standing there looking at those tables, something happened.

The past leapt into the present.

I remembered sitting at those tables as an eighth grader, about a quarter of a century ago, on the cusp of winter break, working with some friends to complete a group project due the following day. This morning, I could almost **see** us there, sitting at the table, like ghosts of Christmas past, much younger ghosts, futures as uncertain as they could possibly be. I imagined approaching that thirteen-year-old kid. I imagined introducing myself. I imagined inviting him to look across the room at his oldest son, now the age he was then, carrying an armload of books to the counter. When I imagined that, the look on his face was priceless. It wasn't happy, or sad. It was **dumbfounded**, because the whole thing is inconceivable to him.

Time is **always** inconceivable.

That eighth-grade ghost looked back at me dumbfounded, because the whole point of life was supposed to be escaping this country town, and here he is, apparently living there once again. The circularity of his life is unimaginable. He looked back at me dumbfounded because his barber is just down the street—a small shop with a spinning red-white-and-blue pole outside of it—and that barber's scissors often get stuck in his thick head of brown hair, but this man standing before him is mostly bald, and what's left has gone from brown to mostly gray. He was dumbfounded by the dark circles beneath this old man's eyes, and the crow's-feet at the edges of them.

The whole thing is inconceivable.

He was dumbfounded by all the loss along the way. For instance, his grandmother is no longer the librarian in this space and is, in fact, no longer alive, taken by cancer just seven short years after that December afternoon. Indeed, he was dumbfounded that all of his grandparents are already gone, and he was dumbfounded that this man in front of him looks far more like them than like him.

The whole thing is inconceivable.

Then, M, the most inconceivable thing of all walked right through the door. You. His future wife. The bearer of his three children. The laugh track to his life. The woman who will become the smile at the center of his world. He was dumbfounded because he can barely look a girl in the eye, let alone take one's hand in marriage. Yet somehow, improbably, here she is.

The whole thing is inconceivable.

If time were an accordion, folding in upon itself, every place containing all moments that have passed through it, so that we could glimpse all of it happening at once, it would be too much for us mortal creatures to bear. To come face to face with our future is to be dumbfounded by the otherness of what we become. To come face to face with our past is to be dumbfounded by the otherness of what we once were.

All of it, inconceivable.

And yet you, my miracle, contain it all. In your laugh lines I can behold my past, in your touch I can feel my present, in your faithfulness I can glimpse my future. Time is made just a little more comprehensible in the person of you. In you, somehow, I can bear the ethereal weight of time. Indeed, in you, that burden gets transformed into something that bears me up—something like awe, something like wonder, something like gratitude.

All these years later, I'm beginning to wonder if that's what marriage is for. Maybe marriage makes time just a little less inconceivable. Maybe marriage is the incarnation of the whole overwhelming, mysterious, terrifying thing, contained in another human body, contained in their memories, contained in the arguments come and gone and resolved and unresolved, contained in years of awkward fumbling beneath bedcovers and those sacred moments here and there when the fumbling somehow became something holy, contained in anniversaries where love was exchanged and anniversaries where fights raged, contained in the grief of the lost child and the joy of the child that arrived, contained in times of plenty and times of scarcity, contained in jobs lost and promotions gained, contained in doctors and diagnoses, contained in pain and ecstasy, contained in milestones and gravestones, contained in mourning and dancing.

Maybe marriage is time with skin on.

Maybe, M, when I embrace you, I come to know a little more of the divine. After all, it is only the divine that can hold time within itself, and for a moment or two here in this mortal flesh, as I hold you, I get to hold all of it, the whole mystery of it folded into this one person, the whole inconceivable thing, right here in my arms.

I think any true companionship can become that kind of container—that kind of holding—but marriage is the only kind of companionship in which we promise to become that container at the beginning, and in which we celebrate having become that container at the end. Maybe that is why we human beings still long for marriage, even though sometimes it is hard and sometimes it hurts. Maybe that is why we howl with grief when it is taken from us by infidelity or by death. Maybe that is why we still stand at marriage altars, the odds stacked against us, the hope of the cosmos alive within us. Maybe that hope is enough.

Maybe it is **more** than enough.

Dumbfounded still,

F

19

TIME ISN'T MONEY,
IT'S MORTALITY

Water is fluid, soft, and yielding.
But water will wear away rock, which is rigid
and cannot yield. As a rule, whatever is fluid, soft,
and yielding will overcome whatever is rigid and
hard. This is another paradox: what is soft is strong.

LAO TZU

YOU HAVE KIND EYES."
I found myself saying these words to a gentleman who attended a talk I gave last spring. When I'm speaking to an audience, I find a face in the crowd that, for whatever reason, feels particularly receptive or encouraging. It's not intentional. It's an unconscious instinct. Over the course of the talk, my eyes may wander across the crowd, but they always return to this one safe face. On that spring evening, my one safe face was an unusual candidate for the job.

He was dressed like a biker, had a handlebar mustache, and was covered in tattoos. It was a talk about how we're all loveable. Mushy stuff. He didn't look like my typical audience. Nevertheless, my eyes returned to him over and over again, and every time it calmed me. After the talk, he approached the book table and introduced himself as Dave. He spoke softly and thoughtfully, and I realized why I had gravitated toward him while I was speaking. There was a kindness in his eyes that is hard to fake. I told him so.

Hearing this, those same eyes began to water, and he thanked me quietly before taking his copy of my book and leaving. When I got home, I told my wife about him. We live in a small town, and I wondered if we might run into each other, maybe even become friends. A week later, his kind eyes were still coming to mind from time to time, when a friend gave me some tragic news. He told me he was close friends with Dave, and I'd made the same impression on Dave that he'd made on me. However, the day after my presentation, Dave had developed seizures. Scans at the hospital had revealed a brain tumor. Doctors had operated. After the surgery, Dave had begun to hemorrhage. Several days later, Dave had died.

I had been imagining Dave and I developing a friendship, but lifelong companionship isn't always up to us, is it? Yes, growing old together is one of the blessed fruits of the long labor of true companionship, but the truth is growing old together requires more than the courage to enter our chrysalis and the commitment to leaving it. It also requires an awful lot of dumb luck. Sure, in true companionship, we learn to cherish the time we have. However, companionship is also at the mercy of time, and time is fickle. That's the folly of *philia*.

Some years ago, a dear couple I once knew finally reached their golden years. After raising three children, after her career as a school administrator, and after his career as a doctor, they were ready for a long, joyful sail into the sunset of their lives. Several months before he retired, he was diagnosed with cancer. Several months after that, he was gone. Companionship is at the mercy of time, and time is fickle. That's the terrible truth lurking at the edges of true companionship.

I know a couple who recently embarked on a fifteenth wedding anniversary vacation. He was a rising star in academia. When they got in the car, they had their entire future ahead of them, and it was bright. By the time they arrived, everything had changed. They checked in to the hotel, he dropped to the ground, and a scan at the hospital revealed a terminal cancer. The opportunity to grow old together is not totally dependent on how badly we want it or how much we're willing to work for it. Companionship is at the mercy of time, and time is fickle. That's the breathtaking courage of it.

When we talk about cherishing our time we are also talking about the passage of time, and whenever we are talking about the passage of time we are talking about our *mortality*. We are talking about how fleeting and capricious the whole thing can be. I think that's why I've been in a funk lately. This morning, I went for a bike ride and took a break along the river that runs through our town. I watched a doe and her two fawns walk slowly toward it and drink from it. I watched a fish jump for its breakfast in the middle of it. I watched hawks circle above it. I gazed at the river, and I saw the cause of my funk. I saw *time*, flowing like a river past me.

Sitting there, I realized I've been in my first midlife funk. According to statistics, I'm past halftime. On average, I've only got thirty-five years or so ahead of me. This year, Aidan, who just yesterday it seems was getting his baby teeth, got his *driver's license*. Last week, Caitlin, who just yesterday it seems was babbling nonsense, shut down a conversation with Kelly by saying, "The past is in the past, Mom, let it go." Quinn, who just yesterday it seems only wanted *LEGOS*, now wants to attend Harvard. In nine short years, Kelly and I will probably be empty nesters. Time is like a river. Its flow is ceaseless. And like any river, time carves a course of its own choosing.

We think of time as soft and fluid, a liquid dimension of existence. In contrast, we think of ourselves and our bodies as solid and substantive, like the earth. We are right on both counts. However, when water flows past a rock for long enough, *the water wins*. In the words of Lao Tzu, what is soft is strong. We human beings are rocks, worn down by the ceaseless flow of time. The next time I renew my driver's license, I'm going to have to switch the hair color on the card from brown to gray.

Gray hair is a sign of time lapping at the riverbank of our bodies.

Even if I stay relatively healthy, my time is short. The next thirty or forty years will pass like a rushing river swollen by spring rains. How can I be so sure? They've already done so once. They will do so again. I hope I get to be here for all of those years, but there is no guarantee that I will. My body might be like the riverbank on the outside of a sharp bend, which bears the brunt of the water's force. The river's current chips away at the earth more quickly there. My body may erode more quickly than I hope. I might not get to grow old with Kelly or, vice versa, she might not get to grow old with me. The list of good people I know who have had to let go of their companionship before it had fully ripened could fill a book of its own. The list of *every* good person who's had to do so is too long to fathom.

I guess what I'm saying is, maybe it's not possible to truly cherish our time without fully *grieving* our time. I knew Dave for about sixty minutes, but the loss of those kind eyes sort of wrecks me. My friend tells me he was a good man, the kind of good man who makes the best of companions. It turns out, what I saw in his eyes was in his heart and in his friendships as well. I think we need to feel the loss of people like Dave in our life. We need to feel it so their passing can be redeemed just a little bit by our renewed ability to truly appreciate our people while we still have them. It doesn't do us much good to get anxious about the river and what it is eroding. We can't control the flow of time. We can only gaze upon it.

We can only cherish it.

20

AND REMEMBER, BODIES MATTER

Good-by, Good-by, world. Good-by,
Grover's Corners . . . Mama and Papa.
Good-by to clocks ticking . . . and Mama's
sunflowers. And food and coffee.
And new-ironed dresses and hot baths . . .
and sleeping and waking up. Oh, earth, you're
too wonderful for anybody to realize you.

THORNTON WILDER

WE CALL KELLY'S GRANDMOTHER VOVO and her grandfather Vuvu. These are the affectionate names by which Portuguese children refer to their grandparents. Vovo and Vuvu emigrated separately from Portugal to the United States when they were children, and they met by chance shortly after they graduated high school. He was enamored of her from the start. She took a little convincing. He was persuasive, though, and they've never looked back. I first met them twenty years ago, shortly after Kelly and I started dating. I watched them dance just a few months later at their fiftieth anniversary celebration. There was something holy about it.

This year, they celebrated their seventieth anniversary.

A number of years ago, Kelly and I decided to tap into their wisdom before it is gone. We sat down one day and asked them their secret to remaining companions for so long. Vovo thought about it for a moment and replied with a question of her own. "We only have one car; how would we get around if we weren't together?" She cackled with laughter at her own joke. Vuvu, sitting beside her, remained quiet. The smile playing at the corners of his lips spoke volumes, though. He still enjoys his bride.

Kelly and I laughed along with them, but then we got serious again. Kelly posed the question a second time. "What is the secret to growing old together?" Vovo once again considered the question briefly and once again responded with a question of her own. "Take a look at us; who else would have us?" Again, she laughed with amusement at her own wit. Again, her groom smiled with delight at his bride. I don't think we ever got a straight answer from them that day, though I think we witnessed their real answer. Their secret to growing old together is playing together.

Several years ago, we were celebrating Vuvu's ninetieth birthday on a warm June evening. He was generally healthy and vibrant, and he'd lived the life of a thoroughly good man. His party was a true celebration. It was playful. Yet, the party was missing music, so I was sent to retrieve my portable speaker. On the thirty-minute round trip, I had time to ponder this man who cared for his granddaughter—the woman I love so much—at a time in her childhood when no other man was around to do so. I'm a words guy, and I wanted to honor him on my return by raising a toast to his heart and soul. For thirty minutes, though, I blanked. I couldn't think of anything I wanted to say about his spirit. It was disconcerting. Then, I realized what was happening. I was overspiritualizing the moment.

I have a tendency to do this because the intangible world—the world of heart and soul and spirit—is important to me. There are extraordinary layers of reality that cannot be experienced with our five senses. We can't smell faith. We can't hold hope. We can't taste love. We can't hear the unity of all things. We can't see the mystery sustaining everything. In this way, spirituality is like eyeglasses for the soul; it helps us to see the unseeable. This is a good thing. It's impossible to touch too much of the untouchable. However, it *is* possible to touch too *little* of the touchable.

We can overspiritualize our embodied lives by overlooking them.

When we overspiritualize our lives, we tend to look beyond time and space and place, beyond blood and sweat and tears, beyond smiles and hugs and homecomings. We scan the horizon of life for something else, and it makes us miss something beautiful. I've done so in the past, and the cost is high. The cost is setting your sights on the heaven outside of time and missing the heaven *inside* of time, the heaven of light and hum and grit and aroma and flavor.

On that June evening, I finally quit overlooking the heaven inside of time when I realized I didn't want to toast him; I wanted to *hug* him. When his days are done, I will, in a way, still be able to speak to him; but once his days are done, I will no longer be able to *hold* him. His soul is as young as it ever was and as young as it will ever be, but his heartbeat of a body is nearly over. His blink-of-an-eye substance will vanish. His fleeting physicality will be finished. Soon, I won't be able to feel the weight of him in my arms. I won't be able to hear him call me "Flanagan" and feel him pull me in close for one more joke from his bottomless supply. Soon, he will fill the world with his spirit, but his reading chair will be empty.

I just wanted to hug him.

It made me think about my wife and my children and my family and my friends. Someday, they, too, will be gone from me, or I will be gone from them. Either way, I will miss them, and more than anything, I will miss their *materiality*. I will miss the flesh-and-blood stuff. The stuff you can only sense with a body. The stuff of light and sound and odor and mass. I will miss the sensation of Kelly's toes finding mine, under the covers, in the darkness. I will miss the feel of Caitlin's fingers as they find mine in a busy parking lot. I will miss the cool, metallic smell of Quinn's hair as the sun slips early beneath the horizon on a crisp autumn afternoon. I will miss the steely strength in Aidan's eyes when he knows he's right and I'm wrong—it's not just spirit; it has a color, a shape, a shimmer, and I will miss all of it.

I will miss the beautiful stuff you can touch, taste, smell, hear, and feel, and I will miss the ugly stuff too. I will miss boogers wiped in out-of-the-way places. I will miss cuts that bleed and scrapes that make showers miserable for a day or two. I will miss the messes my kids make and, hopefully, the messes my grandkids will make. Someday, my body will be gone from theirs, or theirs from mine, and I will miss it all.

For too long, I've thought of the body as a cage, an imperfect, deteriorating container in which our souls restlessly pace, longing to finally be set free. I confess: I've failed to see atoms and cells and tissues and organs and bodies for the gift that they are. I thought the body was the hiding place of the divine; now, I wonder if it is the *completion* of the divine. The *culmination* of the divine.

Souls can feel joy, but only bodies can laugh. Souls can feel sorrow, but only bodies can weep. Souls can feel love, but only bodies can make it. Only bodies can hug. Only bodies can hold each other and tickle each other. Only bodies can snuggle during bedtime books. Only bodies can play in the pool in a strange aroma of chlorine, sweat, and sunblock. Only bodies can splash in puddles together. Only bodies can agree on the best pizza place in town.

Only bodies can feel the air cooling on the night of a nine-tieth birthday party. Only bodies can listen to the strains of Sinatra from a portable speaker drifting on the summer breeze. Only bodies can watch great-grandkids hide-and-seek each other in the gloaming. Only bodies. That's what I will miss. The flesh-and-blood gift. That's what I will miss about Vuvu when he is gone. That's what I will miss about Kelly. That's what I will miss about my kids. That's what I will miss about all of us.

I will miss our time together in this heaven made of molecules and matter.

I hope you won't put *all* of your hope in the heaven after this one. I hope you'll cherish both your time here and the matter we inhabit while we are inside of time. I hope you'll realize this wonderful earth while you are still walking on it. The sound of

21

SO GO
ELDERLY SLOW

The finality of death is meant to challenge us to
decision, the decision to be fully present here and
now, and so begin eternal life. For eternity rightly
understood is not the perpetuation of time,
on and on, but rather the overcoming of time
by the now that does not pass away.

DAVID STEINDL-RAST

O N QUINN'S ELEVENTH BIRTHDAY, while sitting around the dinner table sharing memories of his birth, Kelly shared one I wish had remained forgotten. In the middle of her pregnancy, near the end of a long night at her therapy office, she began vomiting violently. Unable to drive, she called me at my therapy office and asked me to pick her up. I told her to call my mother, because I didn't want to cut my workday short. My mom drove Kelly home, and the next day—on my day off—I took her to the doctor, where she was diagnosed with severe food poisoning and put on intravenous fluids. A trace of bacteria on a handful of alfalfa sprouts might have robbed me of my wife and my already beloved unborn son, but I was focused on other things.

This is more than a little embarrassing, but—given Laura Carstensen's research about the young and the old and the way our values change as our sense of fragility changes—I suppose it is not very surprising. I was young, and I had young-people priorities: achievement and accumulation, speed and expansion. In contrast, if I had allowed the moment to "prime" my fragility—if I had paused for a moment to take in the finitude and uncertainty of it all—I probably would have skipped out on some work to care for my closest companion. When your fragility is primed, you leave the office for your ailing wife.

Several months after Quinn's birthday, our family drove to Boston to celebrate the new year with our friends. As we got closer to their house, the New England traffic got more and more aggressive. Drivers accelerated quickly, darting precariously through small gaps between cars. Everyone appeared to be living in the fast lane. We managed to arrive safely, and the next morning I chose to walk to the nearest coffee shop rather than risk the rush-hour race. As I neared my destination, with cars speeding past me, a road sign caught my attention. Everyone else was ignoring it, but I couldn't take my eyes off of it. It read, "Go Elderly Slow."

Of course, the sign was referring to the speed at which the elderly must drive because of their slower reaction times. However, as motorist after motorist raced past it, I was reminded of that night more than a decade ago when I raced past my wife's troubles with the speed of a young man. I thought about how the pace of the world—both online and offline—has increased so dramatically since then, reflecting the expansive values of the young. I thought about how, more and more, we are racing through life too quickly to notice all the ways our fragility is being primed. As I looked at the sign, I decided right then and there I had a new ambition in life.

I want to go elderly slow.

On a morning not long after we returned from Boston, I had an around-the-clock day at my office scheduled, and I was running late. I was walking out the door with just enough time to get to the office on time, when I heard Kelly holler. Her car battery was dead again. She was driving carpool, so four other families were depending on her, and she needed me to give her a jump-start immediately. I thought about the way I'd sped past her moment of need on the night of her food poisoning, and I thought of all the people speeding past that road sign in Boston. I decided to go elderly slow, and I let myself attend to a truth we often try to ignore.

We are all dying batteries.

Someday, when my vitality gives way to my mortality, I will wish I'd been there for Kelly in her time of need. Within a week, my tardiness at the office will be forgotten. However, in my waning days, these moments that make up my companionship with her will fill my memory lane, and I want that lane to be filled with slow morning walks, not rush-hour traffic. So, I attached the cables, turned on my car, and turned the key in her ignition. Nothing. Her battery was *really* dead. It was going to take a while for it to recharge. It would be elderly slow.

Kelly and I stood there together, two mortal travelers, staring at the machines that carry us on our travels through this world, those machines now linked and exchanging life and energy. As we watched and waited, I pictured our companionship, like a set of jumper cables connecting two souls. I was glad a dead battery had reminded me of our mortality. I was glad I had stayed and gone elderly slow.

Several months after the morning of the dead battery, I retreated to a cabin in the woods to write. It was one of a dozen cabins arranged around a clearing in a state park. Having run out of words for the day, I was sitting in front of my cabin, watching the sun set through the tall pines. To my right, an elderly couple was also sitting in front of their cabin, except they weren't watching the sunset. Rather, they were each staring into a screen. She into her phone. He into a tablet. I silently lamented that even the elderly are succumbing to the fast digital pace of our world. Then, they proved me wrong.

Almost wordlessly, as if they were operating on a wavelength I could not sense, they got up, put their devices down, and joined hands. They began to walk along a path across the clearing, toward the lodge, where they were probably planning to eat dinner. Earlier in the day, I'd crossed that clearing to eat breakfast. Though I was trying to go slow and be mindful, I was also eager to get back to writing, and I'm guessing I crossed it in about thirty seconds. I was not going elderly slow.

This couple was. They both appeared to be hobbled by hip pain or knee pain or both. There was a hitch in their gates, which set a limit on their speed. Hands still joined, they made progress, but slowly. They appeared completely unbothered by this. They took their time, and by the time they finally reached the lodge and disappeared into it, the dying light had almost disappeared from the treetops. Almost everything was in shadow.

Several evenings later, I'm back at home, watching the sun set again.

The sky is a deep, uninterrupted blue, hinting of the autumn to come. The slanted light is glinting off tiny insects in the air. A mower is humming somewhere far, far off. Children are laughing nearby. A dog is barking somewhere in between. Crickets are chirping in perfect concert after a long summer of rehearsals. In the midst of it, as I go elderly slow, there comes the kind of a moment that cannot last forever, and can barely last a moment, but for that moment, everything is okay.

Not the kind of okay that comes from pretending all of it will last. Nor even the kind of okay that comes from believing it will all work out in the end, whatever that may mean to you. Rather, it's a moment of okay that steals over you because you're seeing it all through the eyes of the dead. In other words, *actually* seeing it. Not between texts or Netflix episodes or emails or YouTube videos or phone calls or podcasts or tweets or errands or even thoughts. Not halfway like that. Not like seeing your life as an interruption of your "life." I mean, *truly* seeing it. Looking hard at it, because now that it is over, you know what all of it was worth. Looking not at the big-bad things or the great-good things. After all, you paid plenty of attention to those while you were alive. Rather, looking closely at all those ordinary things you overlooked when you had your chance. Looking long at it, because what else do you have to do now that it is over? And why would you do anything else now that you know?

Like looking at the freckles on your lover's cheek. The light on your little boy's eyelashes. The smudge of ketchup at the corner of your little girl's mouth. The deep, deep brown in the always-rolling eyes of your teenage son. A constellation of bright stars in the night sky or a constellation of brown spots on a ripe banana. A soft weed through hard bricks. Those gnats. Young children playing with each other, old hands holding each other, wrinkles of worry and lines of laughter, the little goodbyes and the little homecomings. The little resurrection every morning upon waking, except that one morning more fragile than all the others, when there will be no waking.

Until then, may we look hard and long, and may we go elderly slow.

22

FEAR (NOT)
MISSING OUT

Time is but the stream I go a-fishing in. I drink at it;
but while I drink I see the sandy bottom and
detect how shallow it is. Its thin current slides away,
but eternity remains. I would drink deeper; fish in
the sky, whose bottom is pebbly with stars.

HENRY DAVID THOREAU

C HERISHING IS ABOUT CHOOSING.
Sure, slowing down creates the space for us to cherish our companions but, if we allow it to happen, our spaces will quickly repopulate with new distractions. Cherishing is about focusing, drowning out the noise, and missing out on everything else that is clamoring for our attention. It's about attending to one or two or a few lovely things to the neglect of so many other lovely things. In other words, cherishing our companions is becoming harder than ever. This is what I mean by that . . .

The iTunes rating system has never really worked. When you view an album in Apple Music, a star appears next to its most-listened-to tracks. This is meant to signify the best songs on the album. Usually, though, the first two or three tracks are starred, regardless of their quality, because with infinite music streaming, we listen to the first few tracks on an album, quickly grow restless, *whether we like them or not*, and then go searching for something else. There is so much content to listen to—and so little time to listen to it all—we don't listen to our music all the way through anymore. This is a variation of a phenomenon so common across digital media that it has its own acronym: FOMO.

The fear of missing out.

Of course, the restless human mind has always struggled to maintain a focus on what is right in front of it, while wondering what *else* might be just around the corner. However, that rest-lessness is now being cultivated and exacerbated by a digital culture that presents us with limitless opportunities to miss out on something, and constant reminders that we are doing so. Teenagers are distraught about not being invited to social gatherings they see on Instagram. Parents feel like failures as they scroll through Facebook feeds full of family vacations they'll never be able to go on. We sit down to enjoy a book on our e-reader of choice, only to discover an hour later that we've spent most of our time searching for another title rather than reading the one right in front of us. FOMO keeps us hunting around rather than settling in. This has consequences.

For instance, it is triggering a "demographic time bomb" in Japan. The population of Japan is predicted to drop from 127 million people to 88 million people by 2065, and to 51 million by 2115. Last year, in Japan, there were less than a million births for the first time in recorded history. Soon Japan will have almost as many senior citizens as able-bodied workers. Japanese economists are terrified. Why is this happening? Are Japanese families simply having fewer children, or is something else going on?

Something else is going on.

The number of Japanese men planning to marry and start families has dropped from 67 percent to 39 percent, and the number of Japanese women planning to do so has dropped from 82 percent to 59 percent. This kind of change is not totally unheard of—over generations and across the centuries, attitudes toward marriage have fluctuated dramatically. However, this change hasn't happened over three centuries or even three generations. It has happened in just three *years*. And Japan is just the canary in the coal mine. We are beginning to see this relationship trend all over the globe. Of course, there are countless explanations for it. Here's mine: we don't listen to our music all the way through anymore, and we don't live our relationships all the way through either.

When FOMO is constantly being delivered into the palm of every hand, it has the power to rapidly transform one of the most fundamental elements of our humanity: our companionship. True companionship requires the commitment to cherish one thing at a time, whether it be in marriage or partnership, families or friendship, neighborhoods or churches. However, when the fear of missing out has taken hold, that kind of commitment feels foolish. Why would we cherish completely this one person or this one place when there are so many other people and places that might bring us even more contentment? Why would we settle for this companion right in front of us when we don't know what other companions might be just around the corner? As FOMO takes over, it seems there is only one thing we *are* content to miss out on: true companionship.

One Sunday afternoon, during my fourth-grade year, I drove my parents nuts.

I'd heard a song on the radio, and I was obsessed with it. I was desperate to get my hands on "She Drives Me Crazy" by Fine Young Cannibals. These days, I would just tell Alexa to play it, but back then you had to scrape together a few bucks, find a ride to your local retailer, and purchase the audiocassette single. It was a whole operation. A project. You had to really commit to it. You had to really want it, and on that Sunday, I *really* wanted it. Unfortunately, I did not have a few bucks. Nor a ride.

Around midday, I started working on my parents. At first, I just dropped hints about how life changing the song was. They didn't get the hint. I asked them if they'd heard it. They hadn't. So, I tried singing it for them. Still oblivious. I dropped a comment about how desperate I was to buy it. Nothing. My dad watched football. My mom prepped dinner. The clock was ticking, so I decided to up the ante. I started to express feelings of distress about not having the song. Nada. Of course, feelings are invisible things, and sometimes you have to add something for the senses. So I started to whine a little. I might have teared up a bit. They were unfazed. I got red in the face. I began to make demands. I decided, if they wanted to keep me from my music, I'd take their afternoon hostage with my behavior. I drove them crazy.

I can't remember which one of them caved. I'm guessing it was my mom. She's fortunate she didn't create a dictator with such decisions. At any rate, with a few bucks in hand, we got in the car, and thirty minutes later I had my cassette single. When we got home, I slid it into my Walkman, pushed play, and listened to it. Over and over and over. I listened to it that day, and the next day, and for weeks. I memorized every word. I learned the song's every nuance. I wore that tape *out*. I cherished it so much, I was afraid of missing out on any of its details. *That* is the fear that frees us up for *philia*.

In 2016, #fomno began trending on Twitter. FOMNO stands for the fear of *not* missing out. It is a way of saying that, if we don't start missing out on some of the digital deluge, we'll start missing out on too much of the life that is right in front of us. When it comes to companionship, we need a little more FOMNO too. We need to fear not missing out on the seven billion other people on the planet, who only distract us from the fleeting time we have with the people who are right in front of us, right here, right now.

The relationships that see us through are the relationships we listen to all the way through.

In true companionship, we make the daily decision to miss out on almost everyone else for the sake of this one beloved person, or these few beloved people. We resist the urge to skip to the next relationship. We go all-in on the companionship we have, rather than constantly wondering about the companionship we don't. We listen to our people over and over again, like a cherished audio cassette, memorizing every word, enjoying every nuance, rewinding, and playing it all over again. Every moment is a cassette player, and every companion is a song. So, let's sit back, press play, and enjoy the music made by those who are seeing us through this one fragile life.

Let's not miss out on any of their details.

23

LAUGH OUT LOUD

*Laugh till you weep. Weep till there's
nothing left but to laugh at your weeping.
In the end it's all one.*

FREDERICK BUECHNER

I AM, BY NATURE, A SERIOUS PERSON. As a young boy, I obsessed about everything that might go wrong and how to avoid it all. I was always very careful to minimize the risk of injury. In church, I'd learn about how Jesus loves me and about how sinners go to hell, and I'd dwell exclusively on the latter. I chose a profession in which I listen all day every day to stories of suffering. I write books about time and mortality. So, yeah, I can be a pretty serious person.

I remember once, in fourth grade, trying to be a little less serious. It didn't work out so well. I'd spent a whole Saturday with some of the older kids in the neighborhood. They'd told a lot of jokes I didn't understand—mostly about stuff I hadn't yet learned in health class—but they'd all laughed extra hard at one in particular, so I figured it must be a good one. The following day, as I sat with my parents in the pew before church, I told it to my mom. I waited for her to laugh the way the older kids had.

I'm still waiting.

Church seemed serious. My parents seemed serious. School seemed serious. *Life* seemed serious. I believe I would have remained that serious boy forever if my companions had not taught me it's okay to laugh, even when life is serious. *Especially* when life is serious. They've taught me, in the words of Frederick Buechner, to laugh until I weep and to weep until there's nothing left but to laugh, because, in the end, it's all one.

In the spring of my junior year of college, my maternal grandmother finally succumbed to lymphoma after a decade-long struggle. She was the grandparent I'd grown closest to over the years. Arriving at her house always felt like coming home. It was a painful loss.

On the morning of her funeral, my uncle decided to distract my brother and I from our grief with a game of basketball in the driveway. While playing, it began to rain ever so slightly. My uncle cautioned us against injuring ourselves on the dampening pavement. Then, while my brother was shooting a free throw and my uncle and I were looking at the hoop and waiting for the rebound, there was a yelp of pain behind us. Somehow, in the safest moment of the game, my brother had jumped just high enough while shooting to land awkwardly and badly sprain his ankle. My uncle started laughing, and he couldn't stop. He's normally a very tender and caring guy, but the circumstances were just too comical for him. It was the contagious kind of laughter too. Soon, I was doubled over in laughter as well. Before long, my brother, despite his pain, followed suit.

It was a bad sprain, and the time before the funeral was spent tracking down bandages and renting a set of crutches for him to get around on. Finally, it was time for the funeral. As the immediate family, we were ceremonially ushered into the church after everyone else had been seated, including my uncle, who married into my dad's side of the family. I'll never forget the moment. As we walked down the aisle, he turned around to watch us, saw my brother hobbling in on crutches, and slowly collapsed into silent laughter once again. His whole body shook.

Watching him laugh, I began to laugh, too, on the inside, where no one could see. I was laughing so hard, new tears sprang to my eyes, this time salty with humor rather than grief. That's how my companions—my grandmother and my uncle and my brother—taught me that laughter can be the silent sound that holds joy and sorrow together. It cannot turn back time and erase loss, but it can magically pause time and *redeem* loss. In the darkest of times, laughter can be a light.

A little more than a year after that funeral, I met my wife. I quickly became addicted to the sound of her laughter. She has a *great* laugh, and I love being the cause of it. So, the first time she took me to Catholic Mass, as we waited for it to begin, I tried a joke in church for the first time since fourth grade. I can't remember what the joke was, but she gasped and admonished me for telling jokes like that in church. "Oh, come on," I appealed to her, "God must have a sense of humor; he created Richard Simmons." This time, she laughed. Success.

When you ask Kelly about our most memorable moments of companionship, she'll tell you about an evening I defended her laughter and the spirit behind it. We were in a chapel rehearsing her sister's wedding ceremony, and her stepfather was giving her a hard time, accusing her of not having a sense of humor. The truth is, Kelly doesn't have a great sense of humor about big people who make small people feel even smaller, which was her stepfather's preferred method of parenting, so he had been mostly on the receiving end of her feistiness rather than her playfulness. As he teased her, I spoke up. I told him she had a great sense of humor. I told him she was one of the funniest people I've ever met. She grabbed my hand and squeezed.

That night, my companionship with Kelly taught me you have to stand up for your laughter.

Laughter doesn't always come easy, and sometimes people want to take it away from you, but they can only do so if you give it to them. So, if you've given your laughter away, go get it back. If you still happen to have your laughter in you somewhere, don't give it up. Surround yourself with companions who want to see it and celebrate it. The Beastie Boys once said you have to fight for your right to party. Sometimes, you have to fight for your right to laugh too. Fighting for each other's laughter is one of the best ways to see each other through.

Over the years, since that first joke during my first Catholic Mass with Kelly, we've laughed as much in church pews as we've laughed anywhere else, always holding it in as well as possible in order to respect the solemnness of everyone around. A recent Sunday was no exception. Aidan was scheduled to lead the congregation in the Old Testament reading for the week, so we arrived early to give him a couple of minutes to review it. When he was handed a slip of paper with the passage on it, he looked at it briefly, turned bright red, and with a wry smile on his face said, "Oh no." He handed us the verse. "When the LORD first spoke through Hosea, the LORD said to Hosea, 'Go, take for yourself a wife of whoredom and have children of whoredom, for the land commits great whoredom by forsaking the LORD.'"

He was fifteen, and in just a few moments, he'd be standing up in front of our mostly elderly congregation saying "whoredom" three times in a matter of seconds. His mother and I could barely contain ourselves. His brother and sister were beside themselves with glee. Moments later, it was time. He walked up to the lectern, cheeks a little rosier than usual, and he started his reading. When he said "whoredom" the first time, we were all grinning. By the third "whoredom," the four of us sitting in the pew were silently and joyfully apoplectic. Aidan says he wants to be a standup comic when he grows up. If he creates material half as funny as that, he'll do just fine.

Perhaps our funny bone had been irrevocably hit. Fifteen minutes later, it was time for the offering. Typically, the kids save a portion of their allowance and contribute it to the plate. This time, they'd forgotten for several weeks, and the contribution was a thick wad of one-dollar bills. As usual, we passed the whole wad down to the person at the end of the row. This time, that person was Quinn. The plate was almost to us when Quinn flattened out the roll, turning it into a stack and, out of nowhere, began to mimic "making it rain," as if he was planning to brush off the bills into the plate with an ostentatious motion. I was caught off guard.

I laughed out loud this time.

The laughter echoed through the silent church, and I immediately choked it down. But it was too late. Our whole family was infected. Aidan shook with the effort of containing it. Kelly had tears running down her face. Caitlin, who doesn't care what she is laughing about as long as she is laughing, had her giggling head buried in my chest. And Quinn just smiled slightly, pleased with himself. The plate arrived, and he simply set the money in it. The good damage was done though. In a church pew, our laughter made a memory of our companionship.

Over time, my companions have taught me that there's an ordinary, boring, repetitive, monotonous, painful, sorrowful, and fleeting life that hangs like a veil over the rest of our beautiful, sacred, holy, eternal, timeless, and mysterious reality. They've taught me it makes sense to be serious about the former, but they've also taught me how to lift the veil so I can get a glimpse of the latter.

They've taught me laughter is the way to see that every bush is burning.

They've taught me that mathematics may be a universal language, but it's not the only one. Laughter is too. It can bridge races and nationalities and cultures. Shared laughter is shared humanity. It accelerates the cultivation of companionship at the beginning. It fortifies companionship over time. And in the end, time can take almost everything away from us except our laughter, if we choose to hold on to it. In the end, laughter can become the soundtrack of *philia*. May we, as companions, over time, become each other's funny bone. May we learn to make the good music of great companionship. May it sound a lot like laughing when you're not supposed to.

24

LET YOUR MEMORIES GATHER

The afternoon knows what the
morning never suspected.

ROBERT FROST

Yesterday, we celebrated the Fourth of July again. We gathered together with friends for hot dogs and hamburgers on the grill. Lee Greenwood sang about American pride through an outdoor speaker. The afternoon was hot and breezeless, so the adults sat in the shade while our kids played in hoses and sprinklers. Then, as our part of the planet spun away from the sun and dusk descended, both generations gathered in the driveway. The kids lit sparklers and the adults lit fireworks. I stood back and took it all in, watching my children enjoy the same holiday tradition I've enjoyed for most of my four decades. I tried to recall some of my own memories of sparklers and fireworks.

But I couldn't.

I couldn't recall a single sparkler or a single big boom, because most *individual* memories are relatively forgettable.

However, memory as a *gathering*—as a collective, as repetition and ritual and tradition, made up of this moment and that moment and a hundred moments like it, as some average of all the sparklers that fizzled and all the sparklers that dazzled, as a union of all the hot and humid and cold and drizzly and perfect and pristine Fourth of July nights, as the sum total of forty years of Independence Day celebrations divided by forty into a quotient of *memory*—that's anything *but* forgettable.

Over time, as memory gathers, it intertwines itself with your soul.

I stood there and watched our kids create an individual memory that will, over the course of months and years, fade away into a hazier whole that is somehow much more than the sum of its parts, in the same way that no grain of sand is very significant but a beach can take your breath away. The kids probably won't remember this specific night on this specific Fourth of July. They won't remember this particular firework that went off, or this particular sparkler that they twirled, or this particular moment with this particular friend in this particular dusk. What they will remember is that around the time of this annual holiday in this small town in this period of their youth, they lit fireworks with their friends while the sun went to sleep, while the fireflies awoke, while their parents looked on and laughed and worried and wondered. This night will get folded into the next one like it, approximately one year from now, and so on, and that folding, that gathering, will feel like something bigger than a boom. It will feel like their *life*.

It's important for us true companions to remember that individual memories are rarely something to write home about. For instance, any given Christmas pageant can be brutal. Half the kids are off key and the other half are lip syncing. It's always too hot in the auditorium. The person behind you has some exceptionally bad breath. The guy in front of you keeps using words usually reserved for R-rated movies. The whole show is running long, and the youngest sibling sitting on your lap is hungry and getting hangry. Somehow, you've got to get them all home and fed and into bed so they can wake up for school tomorrow, and let's face it, you and your companion are probably going to be tired and fighting by the end of it.

However, the *collective* of Christmas pageants is a different story altogether. The average of Christmas pageants—the sum total of each of them divided by all of them—comes out to a quotient that looks less like a grain of sand and more like a breathtaking beach. Somehow, when taken together, my Christmas pageant memories add up to Christmas lights and decorations and an auditorium full of people anticipating something wonderful in the coming weeks. They add up to magic waiting in the wings and companions giving their lives to each other. The average of every Christmas pageant looks like commitment and attentiveness and celebration and delight.

As our memories gather, they add up to something more beautiful than a moment.

We true companions can get way too caught up in individual memories. We want this anniversary to be perfect, or that vacation to be flawless, or this moment of intimacy to be ecstasy, or that attempt at communication to solve everything. Yet, every grain of sand is pretty disappointing. Each grain is just a broken rock, a battered shell. Taken separately, they are as uninteresting as a slug. But be patient. Wait for time to wear down all the rocks, and wait for the waves to beat all the shells, and wait for the tide to push it all together until you have a beachhead. Abide with each other until that happens. Then do this: push your toes into the sand and take it all in.

That's what we human beings are staying together for, what we're struggling for, what we're growing old together for. Not a specific memory, not one good day, but a gathering of all our days. We're forming our portfolio. We're curating the whole of who we are as human beings, as families and friends and couples and companions of every kind. There's something vast and eternal in this gathering. Indeed, the gathering of memory can become so permanent and real it can withstand almost anything.

Even the winds of dementia.

By the time I met my wife's paternal grandfather, he was in the middle stages of Alzheimer's. Kelly loved both sets of her grandparents with a fierceness that made me love them too. I would sit with her grandfather, sometimes for hours, and listen to him tell stories about his life. Sometimes he didn't remember who I was. Sometimes he repeated stories again and again. He was clearly losing most of his individual memories. However, one particular gathering of memory seemed to be holding on to *him*, holding him together even. It was the collective memory of his companionship with Kelly's grandmother.

The last time Kelly and I had lunch with him alone, we took him out to a local seafood place. It was a typical day for him. He mostly remembered who we were and only seemed to forget where we were every once in a while. Then, somewhere in the middle of our soft-shell crab sandwiches, the fog in his eyes lifted and he had a moment of unusual clarity. He smiled and said, "I know I don't remember much anymore, but I remember how much I love Betty, and I know I'm going to be with her in heaven." He couldn't tell you about any specific Christmas pageant or recall any particular sparkler.

He could only recall the big collective boom that was his love for his wife.

Yes, your kids were crabby this morning, and yes, the oldest one was acting more like a teenager than a decent person, and yes, the youngest one acted like she was half her age in order to get attention, and yes, the middle one's missing homework did stress everyone out, and no, you didn't get a cup of coffee until it had already been burned, and no, the dishes did not get done, and yes, you will return to them this evening all crusty and caked on, and no, you did not remember to kiss each other before you all got out the door five minutes too late. These individual memories are grains of sand. Dirty, gritty, and hopefully forgettable. But the *collection* of such mornings? The *gathering* of them? This daily ritual called companionship? Well, it's beachfront property. It's a big boom, and it sparkles in the gloaming. In the end, when all the specifics fade into time and age and neural plaques, even then, it can still make you smile. True companionship is the average of every memory.

It is the only kind of average that is kind of extraordinary.

25

RUST INTO SOMETHING BEAUTIFUL

How many loved your moments of glad grace,
And loved your beauty with love false or true;
But one man loved the pilgrim soul in you,
And loved the sorrows of your changing face.

WILLIAM BUTLER YEATS

MORE RUSTIC SIGNS? I was reading an article on the front page of our regional newspaper about a young entrepreneur program for local high schoolers. At the end of the school year, they'd exhibited their businesses at a career fair. With only a handful of businesses on display, I was surprised to read that two young people had chosen to pursue exactly the same trade. Their businesses would both include salvaging, creating, and selling rustic signs. We live in a small town that can support only so much commerce, and our town *already* has two businesses specializing in rustic signs and repurposed farmhouse decor. Rust is popular these days, it seems.

Typically, when I think about rust, I think about disintegration. I think about old bikes in musty garages and old cars in dusty junkyards. I think of decline and decay. Nevertheless, rust has become one of the biggest trends in home decor. It dominates department store aisles, and it's beginning to dominate the storefronts in our little town. The more I thought about it, the more it puzzled me. Until we visited Vovo and Vuvu.

We pulled into their driveway at the end of a long road trip, and as always, they greeted us by coming outside and meeting us on their front porch. He's past ninety now, and she'll turn ninety next year, so they don't get to the porch as quickly as in years past. They still greet us with smiles and laughter, but beneath the joy there's a palpable fatigue. These trips to the front porch cost them more than they used to.

After hugs and kisses, Kelly and the kids went inside with Vovo, while Vuvu and I went out to his back shed to inspect his failing freezer. In the shed, rusty artifacts littered the floor and hung from the ceiling. We examined the fridge. Though it was set to its coldest setting, the ice cream cartons were soft and sweaty. The refrigerator, too, was showing its age. We decided the food would need to be removed, and we set out for the house to give Vovo the news. On the way, he walked me past his garden. He hadn't planted very much of it this year—some onions and squash and a few tomato plants held aloft by rusty cages. He told me, with resignation in his voice, it would be his last year of gardening. He's been saying this for years, but this time I could hear the finality in his voice. It sounded like grief. It sounded like rust.

We walked back toward the house. He pointed out some bushes and told me he can't do his own landscaping anymore. His grandsons take care of that for him now. He sounded grateful and wistful, all at the same time. Nearing the house, we approached their outdoor shower. He told me that, for the first time in decades, he hadn't turned it on for the summer season. He pointed at the rusty pipes and knobs. It felt like he was pointing at the rust on his life.

We entered the house, and he gave Vovo the verdict on the freezer. The two of them set about rescuing the softening bread and the thawing meat from the rusty old appliance. I tried to help but quickly realized I wasn't needed. The two of them, working more slowly than ever, were still working together. It wasn't as quick or as efficient as it could have been. It wasn't without bickering and disagreement and the kind of muted, loving conflict they've mastered over the last seven decades. Somehow, though, it was *seamless*. It made me think of my recent effort to remove the rusted bolts holding our license plate to our old minivan. When two things rust next to each other long enough, they rust *together*.

Rusted things are almost impossible to separate.

I thought once again of rustic signs. Rust is a sure sign of time passing and matter aging. It made me wonder if we are purchasing so much rust for our homes because we have trouble facing the truth about our rusting bodies and our rusting lives, but we know we need to start trying. I wonder if this unusual trend in home decor is our way of admitting to ourselves that not only is aging good but it is also *beautiful*. I wonder if, as we learn to cherish the truth about our oxidizing lives, we will also learn to cherish the truth about true companionship: it is decorated with rust.

Philia embraces the beauty of aging.

It made me think of how my marriage to Kelly began with the two of us saying things like "from this day forward," "for better, for worse," and "in sickness and in health." In other words, we stood up in front of God and our families and our friends and declared, "We're going to rust, and rust is okay. Rust is part of the gig. Everywhere else in the world, we are in denial about our aging. Here in this marriage, though, we will cherish its beauty. We will enter into it together. On some far-off, distant day, our freezer will die, and our garden will be unplanted, and our outdoor shower will be dry, and we'll figure out together how to solve the next problem life sends our way."

Twenty years have passed since Kelly and I met, and we've begun to rust. Granted, I appear to have been left out in the rain far more often than she has. I have several new age spots I'm told are nothing to worry about. My back isn't what it used to be. I have to be careful lifting things. I have wrinkles at the corners of my eyes. Most of my hair is gone, and the remainder is graying quickly. Kelly and I go to bed earlier now, and we sleep later too. When we wake, we usually ache a little. We don't heal as quickly as we used to. Pulled muscles stay pulled, sometimes for weeks. We are rusting.

So, I'm grateful for two local shopkeepers, two young entrepreneurs, and Kelly's two rusting grandparents who have been showing me that rust is okay. *Better* than okay, actually. Rust can be beautiful. Of course, unlike Vovo and Vuvu, Kelly and I may not get seventy years together. In fact, it's difficult to imagine we will. And that's okay too. We'll take what time we have, cherish whatever opportunity we have to age together, and celebrate the rust we collect along the way. We'll trade the fountain of youth for an old, rusty sign. And we'll hang it right in the middle of our companionship.

26

AND TRADE YOUR STRENGTH WITH EACH OTHER

If you want to go fast, go alone.
If you want to go far, go together.

AFRICAN PROVERB

S HE FLEW PAST ME AND DIDN'T LOOK BACK.
Kelly and I had set out thirty minutes earlier on a bike ride. I'd started out feeling great and ready to ride hard. Kelly, on the other hand, was slowed by problems with her pedal clips, so I slowed down too. Then she got caught at an intersection, and I waited for her to catch up. Then her watch malfunctioned, and I stopped again to help her fix it. I was beginning to get frustrated with the way the ride was going, until I remembered our cycling agreement. On any given stretch of road, the stronger rider is free to lead the way.

So, I began pedaling harder and the gap between Kelly and me widened. At first, I wondered if she would she be angry at me for leaving her behind. It was tempting to slow down and wait for her again. Instead, I decided to trust our agreement. I rode as fast as I could for several miles, down a hillside of hairpin curves, and then pulled over to wait for her so we could climb back up the hillside together. Slowly, she came into view. I assumed she would stop. She didn't. She blew right past me.

I laughed out loud. I could see what was happening here. Now it was her turn to ride strong. I'm generally faster than her on straightaways, and I take more chances going *down* hills, but her strengths include *climbing* hills and endurance. It was her turn to lead the way. I pedaled furiously up that hill, but the gap between us widened. For the rest of the ride, I just tried to keep her in my sights. By the time we arrived home, we were both exhausted and contented because we had cycled the way we have companioned.

We traded strengths.

Life is a long-distance ride that returns you to where you began. While riding that route with your companions, it throws too much adversity at you to expect any one of you to always take the lead. You will have to trade strength along the way. For instance, illnesses happen, first to one companion, then the other. Cold and flu season arrives, and one companion goes down while the other one cooks meals. Then, as the sick one rallies, the helper gets sluggish and feverish. Strength gets traded through chicken soup.

Injuries happen too. Last year, on an early morning bike ride, a pedestrian stepped out in front of me, and I wound up with a torn calf muscle. For a while, Kelly had to take the lead on some things I usually do, like yard work and grocery shopping and pretty much anything you can't do while on crutches. At times, life will give you no choice but to trade strength.

However, misfortune and mishap aren't the only reasons to trade positions. Companions may freely choose routes that require them to change who takes the lead for a while. Careers and vocations and passions come to mind. True companions don't necessarily share the same interests, but they do share the responsibility of supporting each other in *pursuing* those interests. For example, several springs ago, Aidan took the lead in our family during tech week of his first community theater production. Kelly and I supported him with late-night car rides, purchasing tickets for family and friends, and managing last-minute costume crises. A week later, Kelly took over the lead in our family as she ran for her first publicly elected office. We threw all of our emotional and practical support behind her, and she won, and we celebrated together. Finally, a week after that, my first book was published. Kelly hosted a book release party for me, while Aidan skipped a social gathering to stay home with his younger siblings while we attended it.

True companions embrace the trades, both chosen and unchosen.

Of course, there are some long stretches of road that no companions would choose. Steep, steep hills made of diagnoses and diseases. Neurosurgeon and author Paul Kalanithi writes, "Humans are organisms, subject to physical laws, including, alas, the one that says entropy always increases. Diseases are molecules misbehaving." When our molecules misbehave, companions may need to trade strength for a little while, or a long while. Maybe even forever.

I think Vovo's molecules might be misbehaving.

For years, I've been calling her every Thursday afternoon. Until recently, the calls all went pretty much the same way. She would answer the phone and exclaim, "Good afternoon, Flanagan!" and I'd reply, "Well, hello, Vovo!" as if we were both surprised the call was happening. Then we'd talk about their most recent bridge game, our kids, their medical appointments, my writing, their reaction to current events, and on and on and on. In the last few months, though, things have changed. Vuvu has been answering the phone more often than Vovo.

It's a different kind of conversation with him, equally treasured, but mostly focused on politics and his will to stay alive until the current administration is voted out of office. He always makes sure to ask about our kids and to tell me to give his granddaughter a hug for him, but you can tell he's kind of running through a mental checklist. The social stuff isn't his strength. Vovo has always led on that stretch of road. His job was to provide financially, keep life running smoothly, be a supportive companion, and let her take the lead on social matters. Lately, though, Vovo can't remember things.

On our most recent call, Vuvu admitted he's having to do more and more, because his beloved wife can't do it anymore. She used to manage their entire calendar. Now, between making an appointment and hanging up the phone, she can't remember what to write down. Some days they find themselves double-booked, while other days they miss appointments she forgot to record. On this final stretch of road in their companionship, it's beginning to look like they will be trading strength one last time. Vuvu will be leading this final climb.

A little companionship plus a little time will teach you a lot about what it means to be human. It means nothing stays the same, and yet we all return to the same place. It means every parent becomes a child again. It means the strongest person you know will eventually become one of the weakest people you know. It means our molecules will misbehave and, when they do, someone else will have to lead us for a while.

True companionship prepares us to embrace the final trade.

Who knows, that might be the point of the whole hard and hurtful human ride. It might be the reason for every steep hill and every speed bump, every mishap and every malfunction, every long straightaway and every treacherous curve, every illness and injury, every season and setback, every diagnosis and disease, every molecule misbehaving. It might be that, once upon a time, in a place we can't fathom, we were prepared for entry into this world, and while traveling through this world with our companions, we are being prepared for our reentry into that mysterious place. While making countless lonely journeys into ourselves, we are being prepared to ride the very last moment of this human route the only way it can be ridden: alone. While shedding our protections, we are being prepared to conclude the journey with no more baggage than we began it. While cherishing our time, we are being prepared for it to wind down. The final trade is always a hard one. With a little preparation, though, hard things can become holy things.

27

UNTIL DEATH DO YOU PART

Music I heard with you was more than music,
and bread I broke with you was more than bread.

CONRAD AIKEN

Kᴇʟʟʏ'ꜱ ꜰᴀᴛʜᴇʀ ᴅɪᴇᴅ ᴏꜰ ᴀ ʜᴇᴀʀᴛ ᴀᴛᴛᴀᴄᴋ when she was three. She was taken to his gravesite one time in the year that followed. Kelly doesn't remember it, but she's been told she dropped to all fours in agony and clawed at the ground. She was never taken back, and she would not return on her own for another thirty years. Kelly's mother eventually remarried, and that marriage lasted almost three decades. He died too. After burying her second husband, she had no plans to marry a third time. Then, she met a kind man who made her laugh, and she decided to give the light within the light one final try. There was a lot of gallows humor about the third time being a charm.

It was springtime when Kelly and the kids and I loaded up the minivan for the fifteen-hour trek from Illinois to Delaware, to be there for the simple ceremony at the courthouse in Wilmington. Fourteen hours into the drive, as we crossed the Delaware state line, Kelly suggested we show the kids the house where she spent the last years of her childhood. I changed our GPS coordinates. Thirty minutes later, having driven into the middle of nowhere, we came upon the signpost that marks the long driveway to her old home. "Dead End," it reads.

We turned into the drive and a moment later saw what we'd come to see. The old farmhouse had always looked a little abandoned. Now, the abandonment seemed complete. Sagging roof. Peeling paint. Weeds crowding around everything. In contrast, sitting perched atop a hill on the other side of the drive was a small, tidy-looking church. Built in the years after the Revolutionary War, the church has been preserved as a historic landmark. However, our kids were staring at neither. They were gawking at the old graveyard next to the church.

They begged us to walk through it. So, on a bright spring morning full of life and light—nature resurrecting itself all around us according to its ancient rhythm—we went for a walk through the shadow of death. In that moment, it occurred to me, my kids were the embodiment of traditional wedding vows. A marriage begins, on its first day, in its brightest and sunniest moment, full of potential and promise, with two people acknowledging the long shadow of their inevitable ending. "Until death do us part," we say. In a world in which most of us pretend in a million little ways that death will never come for us, every wedding ceremony asks us to remember that it haunts every relationship.

Death is the third wheel in every companionship.

The kids were drawn to some headstones dating back to the eighteenth century, their weathered inscriptions no longer legible. My eyes were drawn to a different kind of stone altogether. They are called companion stones, on which the burials of two marriage partners are inscribed on a single stone. I studied the two dates on each companion stone in the cemetery. No stone had two dates the same. The companions had all died separately. Some dates were close together. Some further apart. However, the most painful companion stones to behold were the stones with only one date of death etched thus far. Somewhere, someone is still alive without *their* someone.

True companionship doesn't usually end all at once; it ends in halves.

For this reason, many people hope to die before their true companions. The idea of living without their lifelong friend is too unbearable to contemplate. I understand where they're coming from. When Kelly dies, the laughter will go out of my life, and I can't imagine getting it back. Nevertheless, I hope I'm the one left behind, because I want to keep my promise. I missed the first twenty-two years of her life, and when we got married, I promised I wouldn't miss another moment of her joy, her sorrow, or any of the ordinary moments in between. I volunteered to become a witness to the numbered days of her life. I don't want her to have to live without her witness.

Eventually, on that bright spring morning, we left the cemetery to complete our journey to Vovo and Vuvu's house, where we stayed for several days prior to my mother-in-law's ceremony. On the morning of her wedding, I picked two rusty shovels from

Vuvu's musty old shed—the one with the rusty fridge now sitting warm and empty—and I put them in the back of our minivan. Vovo and Vuvu got in with us, and I entered our first destination into the GPS. Two hours later we arrived and disembarked. Winter had reasserted itself. The day was gray and colder. The ground soggy and lumpy. Vovo held on to Kelly's arm. Vuvu, cane in hand, made his way slowly around the gravestones. We gathered around Kelly's dad.

Kelly took a shovel, crouched down, and began scraping away the earth that had grown over the stone since our last visit. With the other shovel, I began pushing back dirt too, wishing I could push back time. With a towel, we cleaned the stone, and then we were quiet. There wasn't much to say. There never is. Kelly has few memories of him. She only has memories of *not* having him. He was her first witness, and he was taken from her too soon. I want to live long for a lot of reasons, but most of all, I want to live long so she is not deprived of her final witness the way she was deprived of her first. I want to finish what her dad started.

We returned to the car and entered the destination of the cemetery where Vuvu's family is buried. There we found more gray sky and more gray stones. His parents share a companion stone, with dates about a decade apart. It's a decade more than I can imagine. However, those were not the most tragic dates we saw there. The date on his brother's stone precedes them by many years. He died in a car accident at the age of nineteen. Until death do us part. It's true of marriage, but it's true for true companions of every kind, parents and children and siblings and friends.

We become witnesses to each other, for as long as we are given.

Eventually, we returned to the car and entered the coordinates for the courthouse. After a week of graveyards and companion stones, you'd think the mood in the car would have been somber. It was not. It wasn't even close. There was a lightness of spirit about everyone, in part because death denied is always heavy, but death surrendered to can be as light as a butterfly. It welcomes you into the blessed flow of all things. There is "a time to mourn and a time to dance," proclaims the book of Ecclesiastes. In his own words, Henri Nouwen writes, "Mourning may turn into dancing and dancing into mourning without showing a clear point where one ends and the other starts. . . . Let's trust that the beauty of our lives becomes visible where mourning and dancing touch each other." Mourning and dancing touched as we left a cemetery for a wedding.

Then, an hour later, they touched again as Kelly's mother and her groom made the promise she's already kept twice: until death do us part. As I watched them stand before the justice of the peace, saying their vows, I was reminded of how mourning and dancing touched for Kelly and me, too, at a church altar in October of 2001, as we gladly promised to remain with each other until death does us part. Then, we went dancing. I think they've touched every day we've chosen to love each other in the long shadow of that promise. *Philia?*

Yes, *philia*.

As I watched the justice of the peace pronounce them husband and wife, I recalled another altar I had witnessed just a few weeks earlier. Our family had been standing in one of two lines running down the center aisle of our church. On the altar in front of us, people were kneeling on a cushion, hands lifted, palms up, receiving the bread and the wine. When they finished, they stood up and stepped down from the altar, the lines moved forward, and a new set of parishioners received the next round of Communion. An organist was playing in the background. Our line was moving steadily forward. However, the line next to us was stalled.

At the front of that line was an older gentleman. It was his turn to kneel on the cushion, but a cloud of dementia had passed over his face, and he was at a loss for what to do. Everyone had stopped. They were watching him and waiting patiently for him to remember. In the bread and the wine, I saw the gift of *agape*—the divine and unconditional love at which we all hope to arrive. In this waiting, though, I saw the gift of *philia*. Our lives are a long line moving steadily toward *agape*.

Philia is the love that waits with us.

Philia is a patient witness, and it can be *many* witnesses— those from our past who we have lost, those from our present who we have for now, and those from our future who we will one day come to know. In some mysterious way, as we slowly approach the gift of *agape*, they all stand there in line with us at once. Watching. Witnessing. Waiting. And this waiting is true companionship.

The cloud passed from the elderly man's face. His eyes became animated by memory once again. He took a shaky step forward. He gingerly knelt. He cupped his hands together and raised them, receiving the bread and drinking from the cup. The organ played. It was a celebration of *agape*, but in that moment, it was also a celebration of those gathered there with him, those who waited with him through the cloud of unknowing. It was a celebration of these companions. It was a celebration of this *philia*. In that moment, as he pushed himself up from the cushion with great effort, the organist's music was more than music, and the bread we'd broken was more than bread.

In all moments,

in the midst of your true companions,

your life is more than your life.

A LETTER TO MY WIFE

A Timeless Reunion

Dear M,

Twenty years ago, you promised me we'd figure it out, and for the most part, that's what we've done.

Along the way, we figured out how to add three new companions to our family. Aidan came first, of course, and we've gone out of our way not to miss any of his milestones. Last week, though, he got his driver's license, and his first solo drive was the first of many milestones that can only be a milestone **without** us there. At first, this made me sad and wistful. Then, I remembered again how those monarch butterflies migrate every winter—no one butterfly both departing and arriving. Our companionship with him isn't ending, it's **transforming**. New versions of him and new versions of us will learn how to become companions all over again, and again and again. The name for a swarm of butterflies is a "kaleidoscope."

Every companionship is like an ever-spinning kaleidoscope.

Quinn isn't far behind Aidan. He's twelve now, and after more than a dozen seasons of coaching his soccer teams, I'll have no business coaching in the league he'll advance to next spring. For the first time in his life, I'll be sitting in the bleachers with you, rather than standing on the sidelines with him. It will be a greater distance, and that will be hard, but it will also be a different angle, and that could be beautiful. For instance, I'll get to watch him play while I get to hold your hand. Not only do kaleidoscopes spin, but it is in the tumbling that their truest beauty can be found.

Companionship, too, is at its most beautiful as it tumbles through time.

Of the three kids, though, Caitlin's ten years with us seem to have slipped away most quickly, and it is her slipping away that I resist the most. The truth is, I'm not sure if I could survive something terrible taking her away from us. In a sense, I'd be devastated by her absence, but the truth is, I'd be even more devastated by her continued **presence**. I'd see her in your curls and I'd hear her in your strength. I'd feel her in my **bones**. She's with us now in a way that time and tragedy cannot undo, because our true companions never really leave us.

We carry them around within us forever.

M, lately I've been thinking about our hearts as a gathering space within us. It's a space that exists somehow both within molecules and outside of matter. It inhabits time, but it also transcends time. It's a holy place within us that collects all the companions who have walked with us along the way. Your dad is there, in your gathering space. So are your Vovo and Vuvu, and your Mom-mom and Pop-pop. Indeed, I imagine that holy place within you looks like Mom-mom's back porch in mid-July, salty ocean air wafting through the screens, tables piled high with crabs, fingers slick with butter and gritty with Old Bay seasoning, the air vibrating with the banter of your companions. I think there might always be this kind of timeless reunion happening at the center of all of us.

In my mind's eye, I look into my gathering space, and I see the park along the river on the edge of our town. I can smell charcoal and lighter fluid floating on the breeze. I can hear music playing amidst the low hum of many voices and the occasional punctuation of laughter. It's **your** laughter. I turn in the direction of it and there I see, under a pavilion by the river, the reunion that has been happening within me all along. It's more crowded than I ever imagined it could be. Then, I notice one silver-haired, bowlegged man walking out of the crowd toward me.

It's my Granddad.

When I was a boy, he'd pick me up on summer mornings, take me golfing, and teach me the craft. He was a good teacher. I recall one summer morning when I was even more frustrated than usual, and I started to cry. He looked at me with a mischievous grin and said, "It's so hot out here today your eyes are sweating." In that kaleidoscope of a moment, he was my true companion. Years later, in the summer before he died, he asked me to golf with him several times. I was too busy growing up to take him up on it, and I never got another chance to thank him for his companionship. Now, he stands before me at my timeless reunion and with the same mischievous grin says, "Your eyes are sweating again."

Once a true companion, always a true companion.

My parents are there too. As you know, my relationship with them has been complicated. They've always been a bit of a mystery to me, and I know I've been a mystery to them. All of us just a fingertip out of reach of each other. However, on Thursday nights in the late '80s, while my mom was trying to watch **Cheers**, she'd let me and my brother and sister build a soccer field in the middle of the living room, and she'd quietly enjoy us more than the show we were ruining. Several years later, in the winter of '93, I got my driver's license, and my dad drove around in his in-laws' station wagon for a week so I could drive his old car while he waited for his new one. I haven't thought about those Thursdays and that week for many years.

Moments of true companionship are easy to forget, threaded as they are throughout all the more complicated moments.

Then, I notice that old station wagon my dad drove for a week, and I swivel my head. There she is. My mother's mother. Grandma. When I was with her, the world always felt sane and safe. Her house was the only place I was able to take naps. She'd scratch my back until I dozed, and in my memory it is always summertime, the sun is always out, and a gentle country breeze always blows in through the open window. I'm sure I've idealized her. I think it's okay to honor our lost companions by doing so.

My friends are here too. There's a friend I haven't seen since the second grade. His home was a refuge during a desperately lonely time in my life. And I'm surprised to see a friend I knew only briefly during the fourth grade. He lived right next to the school, and on winter mornings we'd stay warm in his living room until right before the bell rang. I see all the friends who walked with me through middle school and high school and into college. My college roommate is here. He and I walked the bridge from childhood to adulthood together, but we've lost touch over the years. Indeed, I see all the friends who I have left behind and who have left me behind. Our paths have diverged.

I'm suddenly grateful for all the grown-over paths and people who shaped where I am and who I am today.

M, I see another group of friends who you and I have met only recently. There's the friend who checks us for cancer every time a new spot appears on our aging skin. There's the friend who helps us find firewood every fall. There's the friend I call my brother from another mother. There's the friend who takes the deepest parts of me most seriously, and sometimes shows me his depths as well. These are the companions I'll see later this morning in our neighborhood and later today at Caitlin's swim practice. I'm reminded of how much they mean to me. I'm reminded to tell them so.

My eyes continue to roam and, scattered throughout the crowd, I see faces I don't recognize. They, however, look at me like they've known me forever. I'm momentarily confused until, in their gaze, I recognize the truth: they are the companions I have not yet met. They are the friends that the river of time will sweep into my life and deposit here, within me. I think I'm going to be more intentional about waiting for them, watching for them, and welcoming them.

You never know when more philia will arrive.

Then I hear it again. Your laughter. I turn and I see you, my truest companion, weaving in and out of the chattering crowd, making each of them feel at home through your deep presence, in just the way you have made me feel at home for the last two decades.

Twenty years ago, I began calling you "M" because it was miraculous to me that you had not only survived but **thrived** within the story you were given. It was miraculous to me that you had arrived at the intersection of our lives so whole and so good. Now, though, I call you "M" for a new reason. Now, I call you my miracle because the whole of our companionship has equaled more than the sum of its parts. With you, the bread we've broken has been more than bread and the music we've danced to has been more than music. With you, my life has been more than my life. With you, one plus one has equaled a thousand.

With you, figuring it out has always been the most miraculous way to make my way through.

Timelessly,

F

ACKNOWLEDGMENTS

*I*N THE CHAPTERS OF A BOOK, there is never enough room to describe everyone who has shown up at your inner reunion, though in the acknowledgments you get a little more space to do so. My agent, Kathy Helmers, is there at my inner reunion. I was determined to write a very different book, and Kathy, with her characteristic grit and grace, convinced me to write this one. As always, she was right. Thank you, Kathy, for being the guiding light of my literary life.

I'm grateful for everyone at InterVarsity Press, especially my editor, Cindy Bunch, who jumped at the chance to publish this book and who has maintained that same level of support and enthusiasm throughout, shepherding this work so wisely from start to finish. Thank you, Cindy, for inviting me into the IVP family.

In a way, writing is still my side gig, and I'm grateful for the therapists at Artisan Clinical Associates who walk with me every week through the rest of what I do as a clinical psychologist. Miranda, Rory, and Ben—Artisan is a special place because of you.

This book was shaped over and over again by the vulnerability and wisdom of my online tribe. We gather as many Fridays as we can on Facebook Live for our Human Hour conversations, and your feedback during those discussions was critical in shaping the first part of this book. Thank you, thank you, thank you. See you on Friday.

Similarly, the fingerprints of Westlake Hills Presbyterian Church in Austin, Texas, are all over this book. I beta-tested all of these ideas with you at your marriage retreat in January 2020, and your honest feedback put the finishing touches on all of it. Thank you for sharing your wisdom with me.

There are more companions at my inner reunion than I could ever list, even in this extra space. However, I feel a special tenderness for those who gathered with me at Thanksgiving during my childhood. My aunts and uncles and cousins and siblings. I don't spend very much time wishing to be a kid again, but if I were ever to return to those days, I'd hope to return to those seventy-two hours every year, when we gathered as companions and shared that holiday with one another.

Finally, of course, I want to say thank you to my truest companions, with whom I finished this book while we were under quarantine together. For a lot of reasons, I wanted that quarantine to end as soon as possible, but for four reasons, I wanted it to last forever. Aidan, Quinn, and Caitlin, I don't just love you; I *like* you so very, very much. I'd be grateful to go through anything with you. And M, we can now add "pandemic" to the list of things we've figured out together. I still can't believe you let me say all of this in public. It is the single most loving gift anyone has ever given me. Now more than ever, you are more than my true companion.

You are my miracle.

NOTES

WHAT YOU NEED TO KNOW

8   *The moon looks wonderful*: Marilynn Robinson, *Gilead: A Novel* (New York: Picador, 2004), 119.

16   *that breakfast scene in the Bible*: John 21:1-19.

19   *We're all just walking each other home*: Ram Dass, ramdass.org /ram-dass-quotes/.

1: ABANDONMENT IS NOT LONELINESS

27   *You are not dead yet*: Rainer Maria Rilke, *Rilke's Book of Hours: Love Poems to God* (New York: Riverhead Books, 1996), 61.

2: NEITHER IS SHAME

33   *Loneliness happens*: Kelly Flanagan, *Loveable: Embracing What Is Truest About You So You Can Truly Embrace Your Life* (Grand Rapids, MI: Zondervan, 2017), 113.

4: A CAUTIONARY NOTE ABOUT THE DIGITAL CROWD

43   *Around 2012, something happened to teenagers*: Jean M. Twenge, PhD, *iGen: Why Today's Super-Connected Kids Are Growing Up Less Rebellious, More Tolerant, Less Happy—and Completely Unprepared for Adulthood* (New York: Atria Books, 2018), 93-118.

5: YOU ARE A GREAT AND PRECIOUS THING

52   *faith is confidence*: Hebrews 11:1.

6: SO LEARN HOW TO BE ALONE

56   *In 1949, professor of literature*: Joseph Campbell, *The Hero with a Thousand Faces: The Collected Works of Joseph Campbell* (New York: Pantheon, 1949).

60   *As hard as it is to believe*: Henri Nouwen, *Reaching Out: The Three Movements of the Spiritual Life* (New York: Doubleday, 1975), 34.

7: MAYBE EVEN FIND GOD IN IT

68 *praying ceaselessly*: see 1 Thessalonians 5:17.

69 *It is in the midst of the chaotic suffering*: Henri Nouwen, *The Genesee Diary: Report from a Trappist Monastery* (New York: Doubleday, 1981), 180.

Surely, the LORD *is in this place*: Genesis 28:16.

from an ancient hillside: see Matthew 5:1-12.

Earth's crammed with heaven: Elizabeth Barrett Browning, *Aurora Leigh* (New York: Oxford University Press, 1993), 246.

70 *the kingdom of heaven is near*: see Matthew 3:2.

A transfiguration with just a few onlookers: see Matthew 17:1-3.

on the Mount of Olives: see Luke 22:39-44.

the loneliest of crosses: see Mark 15:34.

72 *In these moments of solitude*: Paul Tillich, *The Eternal Now* (New York: Scribner, 1963), 24.

the narrow way: see Matthew 7:14.

8: AND LET SOMEONE STAND WITH YOU FOR AWHILE

75 *the feeling of lacking or losing companionship*: "How the World's First Minister Will Tackle 'the Sad Reality of Modern Life,'" *Time*, April 25, 2018, https://time.com/5248016/tracey-crouch-uk-loneliness-minister/.

A LETTER TO MY WIFE: LOVE GOES THE LONG WAY

86 *As a man named Paul*: see Romans 7:15-20.

9: OBSERVE YOUR PROTECTIONS

92 *plank in your own eye*: see Matthew 7:3-5.

93 *great love or great suffering*: Richard Rohr, *Yes, And...: Daily Meditations* (Cincinnati, OH: Franciscan Media, 2013), 302.

10: ANGER

99 *It might be over soon*: Bon Iver, "22 (Over Soon)," *22, A Million*, Jagjaguwar, 2016.

100 *perfect love drives out fear*: 1 John 4:18.

When we were children: Madeleine L'Engle, *Walking on Water: Reflections on Faith and Art* (New York: Penguin Random House, 2016), 182-83.

11: PEACEFAKING

104   *at the age of twelve*: see Luke 2:41-52.

talked back to his mother: see John 2:1-12.

religious authorities demanded answers: see Matthew 15:1-3.

of being hypocrites: see Matthew 23:13-36.

fashioning a whip: see John 2:15.

12: CERTAINTY

110   *Therefore everyone who hears these words*: Matthew 7:24.

14: COMPETITION

123   *We do not want merely to see beauty*: C. S. Lewis, *The Weight of Glory* (New York: HarperCollins, 2001), 42.

16: FIXING

136   *Care is something other than cure*: Henri Nouwen, *Bread for the Journey: A Daybook of Wisdom and Faith* (San Francisco: HarperOne, 2006), 47.

137   *Jesus wept*: John 11:35.

17: HELICOPTERING

140   *a parent who takes an overprotective*: "OED adds 'babymoon' and 'helicopter parenting' to the dictionary after consulting Mumsnet," *The Telegraph*, January 30, 2018, https://telegraph .co.uk/news/2018/01/30/oed-adds-babymoon-helicopter-pa renting-dictionary-consulting/.

143   *soul is overwhelmed with sorrow*: Mark 14:34.

his sweat fell to the ground: Luke 22:44 NLT.

Father, if you are willing: Luke 22:42 NLT.

My God, my God: Matthew 27:46.

PART 3—GROW OLD—CHERISHING YOUR TIME

153   *In his bestselling book*: Atul Gawande, *Being Mortal: Medicine and What Matters in the End* (New York: Metropolitan Books, 2014), 94-99.

154   *horizons are measured in decades*: Atul Gawande, *Being Mortal*, 97.

life's fragility is primed: Atul Gawande, *Being Mortal*, 99.

20: AND REMEMBER, BODIES MATTER

166   *Several years ago, we were celebrating*: "What I Will Miss When They Are Gone," *UnTangled*, July 18, 2017, https://drkellyfla nagan.com/2017/07/18/what-i-will-miss-when-they-are-gone/.

22: FEAR (NOT) MISSING OUT

178   *demographic time bomb*: "Japan's Demographic Time Bomb Is Getting More Dire, and It's a Bad Omen for the Country," *Business Insider*, June 5, 2018, https://businessinsider.com/japans-popu lation-is-shrinking-demographic-time-bomb-2018-6.

180   *I was desperate to get my hands on*: Fine Young Cannibals, "She Drives Me Crazy," *The Raw & the Cooked*, London Records, 1988.

23: LAUGH OUT LOUD

187   *When the LORD first spoke*: Hosea 1:2 NRSV.

25: RUST INTO SOMETHING BEAUTIFUL

195   *How many loved your moments of glad grace*: William Butler Yeats, *The Collected Poems of W. B. Yeats* (London: Wordsworth Edi- tions, 1994), 62.

26: AND TRADE YOUR STRENGTH WITH EACH OTHER

201   *Humans are organisms*: Paul Kalanithi, *When Breath Becomes Air* (New York: Corcovado, 2016), 70.

27: UNTIL DEATH DO YOU PART

204   *Music I heard with you*: Conrad Aiken, *Selected Poems* (New York: Oxford University Press, 2003), 271.

208   *a time to mourn*: Ecclesiastes 3:4.

Mourning may turn into dancing: Henri Nouwen, *Bread for the Journey: A Daybook of Wisdom and Faith* (San Francisco: HarperOne, 2006), 97.

ABOUT THE AUTHOR

KELLY FLANAGAN is a writer, speaker, and clinical psychologist who enjoys helping people cultivate true companionship and a true calling with their most authentic self. He is the founder of Artisan Clinical Associates in Naperville, Illinois, a therapy practice serving the needs of individuals, couples, and families in the Chicagoland area. He is a sought-after speaker to churches, marriage retreats, hospital systems, corporate leadership, entrepreneurs, and professional sports teams, and he hosts an annual private retreat focused on personal formation and relationship health.

In 2005, Kelly earned a PhD in clinical psychology from Penn State University and went into private practice. In 2012, he began his now-popular blog at drkellyflanagan.com, which has reached millions of readers. He continues to blog monthly about topics related to personal growth, spiritual formation, and relationship flourishing. His writing has been featured in *Reader's Digest* and *The Huffington Post*, and he has appeared on *The Today Show*. In 2017, he published his first book, *Loveable: Embracing What Is Truest About You So You Can Truly Embrace Your Life*.

Kelly is married to another clinical psychologist named Kelly, and their three children are in the eleventh, seventh, and fifth grades. They live in a small, rural town outside of Chicago, where they are learning to slow down, be present to one another, and enjoy their companionship while they can.

**To connect with Kelly, go to his
website at drkellyflanagan.com, where you can
subscribe to his monthly newsletter, contact him for
speaking, and get your free copy of his fifty-two-week plan
for embracing your most authentic self, cultivating true
companionship, and clarifying your calling.**

ALSO AVAILABLE

True Companions
Study Guide
978-0-8308-4770-9